FONDA
HER LIFE IN PICTURES

JAMES SPADA

A DOLPHIN BOOK

DOUBLEDAY & COMPANY, INC., GARDEN CITY, NEW YORK 1985

Designed by Laurence Alexander

Library of Congress Cataloging in Publication Data

Spada, James.
    Fonda, her life in pictures.

    "A Dolphin book."
    1. Fonda, Jane, 1937–   —Portraits, etc.
I. Title.
PN2287.F56S6 1985   791.43′028′0924 [B]   85-1534
ISBN 0-385-18827-7
Library of Congress Catalog Card Number 85-1534
Copyright © 1985 by James Spada

Books by James Spada

Fonda: Her Life in Pictures
Shirley and Warren
The Divine Bette Midler
Hepburn: Her Life in Pictures
Judy and Liza
Monroe: Her Life in Pictures
Streisand: The Woman and the Legend
The Spada Report
The Films of Robert Redford
Barbra: The First Decade

Acknowledgments

For their generous help in the preparation of this book, many thanks to Ben Carbonetto, Fred Lawrence Guiles, J. Watson Webb, George Zeno, Michel Parenteau, Bob Scott, Frank Teti, Bob Deutsch.

For their friendship and moral support, an affectionate nod to Dan Conlon, Chris Nickens, Paul O'Driscoll, Steve Macofsky, Ken deBie, John Cusimano, John Ruggles, Karen Swenson, Guy Vespoint, George Schulman, Michael Schwerin, and my family.

For their professional and personal generosities, thanks to Kathy Robbins and Richard Covey, Loretta Fidel, Paul Bresnick, Jack Dwosh, Laura Van Wormer, Larry Alexander, and Doug Bergstreser.

For Richard and Carla Spada

CONTENTS

FONDA

PART ONE

OFFSPRING
1937-59

Jane at four and a half, spring 1942.

When Henry Fonda's first child, Jane Seymour Fonda, was born on December 21, 1937, he had not yet given one of the classic American performances in *The Grapes of Wrath*, nor, in fact, had he achieved leading-man stardom—the release of *Jezebel* didn't come until two and a half months after Jane's birth. Her nickname "Lady Jane" wasn't, as some later thought, a reflection of her father's position in the Hollywood aristocracy, but rather of the ancestry of her mother, Frances Seymour Brokaw, whose forebear Lady Jane Seymour was the ill-fated third wife of King Henry VIII. The significance of her nickname meant little to Jane; a rambunctious tomboy by the time she was five, she hated being called the "sissy" name.

By this time, Henry Fonda—who himself boasted royal ancestry—was indeed one of Hollywood's princes. The life-style of his family, which now included a son, Peter, born in February 1940, was appropriate—they lived on an elaborate estate high atop a Brentwood hill, with fabulous views, tennis courts, a swimming pool, and acres of land.

Jane was unimpressed with the trappings of her father's stardom, but she was awestruck by the man himself. Her entire early life, she has said, was motivated by a desire to please him, gain his approbation. It was not easily done; often, in fact, it was difficult just to get her father's *attention*. Henry Fonda was a man who hid his emotions at all times, who was embarrassed by outward displays of affection, and who frequently said nothing to his children—both Jane and Peter can recall long motor trips without a word being exchanged with their father.

Henry's natural reserve toward his children was exacerbated by his wife's neurotic obsession with protecting them. He acquiesced to Frances's regimental dictates, which included isolating Jane. "I would have liked to play with her and pamper her," Henry told his biographer, Howard Teichmann, "but the nurse was strict . . . I needed permission to see my own baby. Jane was quarantined. I often had to put on a mask when I went to see my kid, not because I had a cold, it's just the way the nurse and Frances wanted it. It makes me sad when I think about it. She grew up without ever being hugged or fondled. I choke up when I remember what I missed and what she missed."

Like many men who repress their emotions, Henry Fonda was prone to explosive anger. Jane has said, "I was terrified of his rages. That didn't necessarily mean I always behaved, but I was very scared of his disapproval . . . no one explained to me that it was really himself that my father was angry with, and so I would blame myself or my brother . . ."

Jane found little more comfort or loving from her mother. "I didn't like her near me," she said. "I didn't like her to touch me because I knew she didn't really love me . . . My mother already had a daughter [from a previous marriage] and wanted a son, but had me instead." She was told by her grandmother that if Frances's third child—the last she would be able to have, according to her doctor—had not been a boy, she was planning to adopt one immediately. When Peter was born, Jane says, "She didn't have to worry, she had a son . . . and she preferred him, I believe."

Just before Jane's fifth birthday, her father enlisted in the wartime Navy. He was away for three years, and when he returned she grew more distant from him than ever—mainly because he himself felt alienated from his family. His children, he felt, were becoming more and more influenced by his wife rather than by him, and Frances had become fanatical about appearances and the way things "should be." Fonda withdrew even further from his wife and children.

In 1948, Henry scored a major success on Broadway in *Mister Roberts*, and when it became clear that the play's run would be a long one, the family moved to Greenwich, Connecticut. Jane and Peter were both quite unhappy about it. They had loved the family estate, Tigertail—especially Jane, who could run around its woodlands in her cowboy hat and boots, blithely ignoring the protestations of her mother to be more "feminine." In Greenwich's social structure, etiquette was paramount, and living there provided Frances with the opportunity to mold her daughter into a "proper young lady." But Jane would have none of it. She was developing a strong rebellious streak, and frequently got into trouble. She was popular at school, but her classmates' parents weren't pleased: they accused Jane of being a "bad influence" on their children. She reportedly told "dirty traveling salesman stories" in an abandoned shed, and she was thrown out of her Girl Scout troop.

Much of Jane's behavior resulted from her growing confusion about her parents' relationship. Henry and Frances had become so estranged that he rarely made the trip up from Manhattan after an evening's performance. Early in 1949 Henry confirmed to Frances something she had suspected: he had fallen in love with Susan Blanchard, the twenty-one-year-old stepdaughter of composer Oscar Hammerstein II, and wanted a divorce.

The admission was a body blow to a woman who had been descending into severe depression for several years; she had, for months, refused to leave her bed, withdrawing from everyone around her. Frances's depression was deepened by the prolonged dissolution of her marriage, the death of her daughter Pan's newborn baby, and her conviction that she would never again find a man willing to marry her.

In this last regard, Frances was a victim of her time as much as of her own neuroses. Like many of her contemporaries, she was a bright, able woman whose sense of self-worth revolved around her husband. Her identity was drawn from being Mrs. Henry Fonda, and when she was faced with the prospect of losing that identity, she was unable to see any life beyond. At forty—eight years younger than her strikingly fit and beautiful daughter is now—Frances saw herself as old, a faded beauty whose husband was leaving her for a younger woman.

Frances suffered a nervous breakdown, and was committed to a sanitarium, where, in April 1950, she killed herself. The children were told that their mother died of a heart attack. "I sat on the edge of my bed," Jane said, "and wondered why I couldn't cry."

A few months later, Jane discovered the real cause of her mother's death by reading a movie-magazine article about her father. At summer camp shortly thereafter, she often woke up screaming in the middle of the night; the entire staff would be needed to calm her.

When her father married Susan Blanchard in December 1950, Jane became closer to Susan than she had been to her mother. Just nine years older than Jane, the beautiful, sophisticated Susan was like a big sister. Jane idolized her new stepmother: "Susan was everything I wanted to be!" And Susan, rather than resenting her stepdaughter, taught the thirteen-year-old budding young woman about fashion, makeup, carriage. "She put in a lot of time with us," Jane says. "Thinking back, when I realize how young she was, I appreciate her even more."

Susan's influence and Jane's own maturing ended her tomboy phase, and the influence of Connecticut society turned Jane into a sophisticated, well-turned-out young lady. She attended the Emma Willard School in preparation for Vassar, and developed a sense of elegance and style that set her apart even from her society-girl classmates. But her rebelliousness was, if anything, stronger than ever—and it would soon take forms that greatly alarmed Henry Fonda.

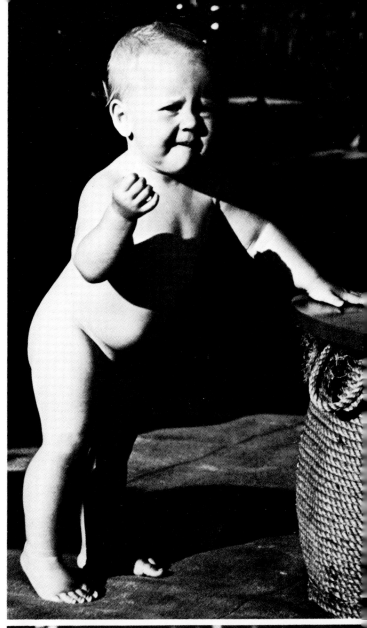

TOP RIGHT Jane takes her first tentative steps at six months, summer 1938.

BOTTOM RIGHT Jane and her half-sister, Pan Brokaw, wear identical outfits, early 1939. Pan's father was George Brokaw, a millionaire and former New York congressman who had married the much younger Frances Seymour after his divorce from Clare Booth; he had left his young widow and daughter millions in his will. Although Pan and Jane got along, they apparently were not very close.

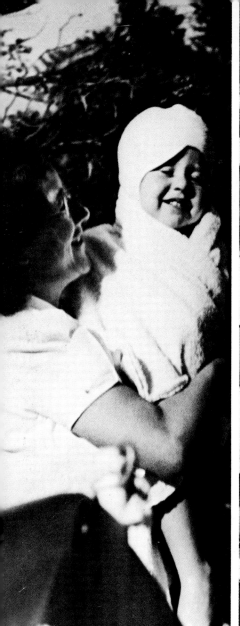

Jane's nurse, Mary, bundles her up after a swimming lesson from her father, summer 1939.

Dressed again after her swim, Jane smiles for the camera along with her father and (left to right) cousin Prudence Peacock, a neighborhood friend, and aunt Harriet Peacock, Henry's sister.

Frances Fonda poses with her children on Jane and Peter's christening day, June 23, 1940. Henry, not a religious man, agreed to Frances's request for the christenings only if both could be done on the same day, with a minimum of fanfare. The children's godfather was Frances's friend J. Watson Webb, Jr., a photographer who took pictures of the Fonda children whenever possible, and who took most of those in this section.

Jane plays to Watson Webb's camera after the christening.

5

At the first Fonda family home at 255 Chadbourne in Brentwood, Jane tries her hand at painting (an avocation diligently pursued by her father). Spring 1942.

Watson Webb captures Jane at play later the same day.

OPPOSITE A studio portrait of an angelic Jane, fall 1942.

Christmas 1943: The Fonda family pose at Tigertail. Henry is on leave from his navy duties.

ABOVE Summer 1943: Henry explains the dynamics of sailing to Jane using a miniature sailboat in the family pool at their new home on Tigertail Road in Brentwood. By the time she was five, Jane had begun to express interest in many pursuits traditionally considered masculine. Henry was more than glad to encourage her.

11

Easter Sunday 1944: Jane and Peter wear outfits made from identical material. By this time, Jane had become a rambunctious leader for her brother and her playmates. Brooke Hayward, the daughter of agent Leland Hayward and actress Margaret Sullavan (Henry's first wife), was Jane's best friend—the Haywards were neighbors in Brentwood, and later followed the Fondas to Connecticut. Brooke recalls that "it pleased her to have other kids following her, even if most of the time it was only her little brother." Their favorite game was cowboys and Indians, as Jane led noisy raids on Indian forts and protected their own fortress from attack.

OPPOSITE The Fonda family are reunited after Henry's return from the Navy, 1945. Frances, left, and her look-alike daughter Pan play with the family dog. Tomboy Jane, seven, wears a shirt similar to those of her brother and father—who still sports his military crew cut.

ABOVE RIGHT Jane serves as a flower girl at Pan's wedding in 1949. Pan married her young art instructor, Bun Abry, but the union, rent by the death of their baby, did not survive.

Immediately upon her graduation from the Emma Willard School in June 1955, Jane performed with her father for the first time, in an Omaha Community Theater presentation of Clifford Odets's *The Country Girl.* Henry was reluctant to allow Jane to appear as an ingenue in the play about an alcoholic actor and his wife (Dorothy McGuire, pictured) because he felt he wouldn't be able to handle such a difficult part *and* worry about Jane. But when his sister Harriet—a strong supporter of the playhouse, which needed the Fonda name to help raise money for a new building —assured him that she would take care of Jane, he agreed.

Although the play was scheduled for just a one-week run, the publicity surrounding the union of three Fondas (Peter worked backstage) helped raise a great deal of money for the playhouse. Henry recalled being quite impressed with Jane's acting ability: "In one scene, Jane had to enter crying. That isn't easy—walking on at the height of an emotional breakdown. I didn't want to watch. I didn't think she'd be able to handle it . . . well, Jane came on wailing and wet-eyed . . . I couldn't believe it. I couldn't believe she was acting. I thought all her anxieties had broken through the Fonda façade and come tumbling out. But the minute she cleared the stage her face relaxed, she looked at me and said, 'How'd I do?' "

Later Jane revealed the technique she had used: "I asked one of the stagehands to whack me around, to slap me hard, and that, plus the petrifying fear and trembling I had of acting on the same stage with my father, turned the trick."

OPPOSITE Immediately after their week-long stint in Omaha, Peter, Jane, and Henry were joined by Susan Fonda and newly adopted baby daughter Amy for a trip to Rome, where Henry was to film *War and Peace.* While in Rome, Susan told Henry that she was planning to get a divorce. A month later, she returned to New York with the children. Before Henry left Rome following completion of filming, however, he had met the woman who would become his fourth wife, Afdera Franchetti, the twenty-four-year-old daughter of a Venetian aristocrat. On March 10, 1957, Henry married Afdera, but neither Jane nor Peter grew to like her; she lacked maternal instinct and gave them —and Henry—little of her time, apparently preferring parties and heavy rounds of socializing to the domestic tranquillity her husband, now in his mid-fifties, preferred. They were divorced early in 1961.

14

PART TWO

SEX KITTEN
1960-64

Jane is her most sex-kittenish in this publicity portrait for the 1962 film *Period of Adjustment.*

During the fall of 1955, Jane Fonda entered Vassar, the venerated women's college in Poughkeepsie, New York. She despised its regimentation and finishing-school atmosphere, and begged her father to let her quit. When he refused, her behavior became erratic; there were reports that she raced a motorcycle through the corridors of her dormitory, that she was running with a daring and sexually loose crowd. "When I discovered that boys liked me, I went wild," Jane said. "I was out all the time. I never studied." Her grades dropped, she missed curfews—once staying away all weekend, a serious breach of the regulations—and she did everything she could to force the school to expel her. They didn't oblige.

Henry, concerned with the behavior of both his children (Peter had become heavily involved with drugs), agreed to send Jane to the Sorbonne in Paris, where she said she wanted to study art; at this point in her life her professed desire was to be an artist. But once she got there, painting was the last thing on her mind. "I lived there for six months and never opened my paints," she said. "I was nineteen, an age when you know you are not happy but you don't know why, and you think a geographical change will change your life."

Instead, her behavior in Paris became an extension of her life at Vassar, although it was quite a bit more sophisticated. She became involved with a bohemian, intellectual crowd which championed the supremacy of the mind while allowing full sexual expression to the body. When Hank Fonda began hearing stories of his daughter's Parisian escapades, she was quickly brought back to live in his New York apartment with him and Afdera.

Early in 1958, Henry Fonda was filming *Stage Struck*, a remake of *Morning Glory*, the 1933 film that won Katharine Hepburn her first Oscar. His costar was Susan Strasberg, the daughter of the legendary Actors Studio guru, Lee Strasberg. Jane and Susan became friends, and Jane became fascinated with Susan's father and his celebrated Method acting theories. Strasberg and his wife Paula had trained Marlon Brando, Maureen Stapleton, James Dean, Paul Newman, Joanne Woodward, Marilyn Monroe, Geraldine Page, Anne Bancroft, and dozens of other world-renowned actors, teaching them to use their own inner lives and experiences—"sense memory" —to draw from themselves the emotion they needed to create a character and give a performance. By now, Jane was beginning to feel that she wanted to act, and she applied for one of Strasberg's private classes—there was no possibility at this point that she would be admitted to the school itself.

She spoke first to Paula Strasberg, then to Lee. "The only reason I took her," Strasberg later said, "was her eyes. There was such panic in her eyes." Jane was indeed terrified of this new commitment— especially since she was treading in the hallowed footsteps of Henry Fonda. But she felt a stronger excitement about acting than she had ever felt before, and Strasberg soon saw that she was more than just a frightened young girl. "The first time I did something in front of the class," she said, "Lee Strasberg for some reason stopped me and I don't know what he said, but he was complimenting me and said he saw a tremendous amount of talent, which absolutely changed my life. Nobody had ever told me that I was ever good at anything."

Studying with Strasberg opened up a whole new world for Jane Fonda, and channeled her energies and excitements and ambitions into the acting life. But her father was unimpressed by Strasberg's encouragement of his daughter. Although he had seen potential in Jane in *The Country Girl* and several school plays she did, he never told her. He had publicly lambasted Strasberg's Method approach as "useless garbage," and when Jane excitedly told him about some new breakthrough or a compliment from Strasberg, he would express no interest whatsoever. His seeming indifference to her further confirmed her ambition to amount to something in her father's eyes—and led her into a series of relationships with men who could nurture her dreams the way her father did not.

Jane's first serious relationship was with Timmy Everett, a young singer/dancer/actor classmate who already had several Broadway shows to his credit. Although he was slight and boyish, and their relationship was based in large measure on physical attraction ("Jane used to say how much she loved my body"), he had tremendous authority when it came to performing. He was experienced and talented, and he became Jane's mentor and manager as well as her lover. But after a year and a half, Jane met someone stronger, more theatrical and more authoritative than Everett—Andreas Voutsinas.

Voutsinas was a disciple of Strasberg's, an aspiring director and acting coach, and he played the role to the hilt. His clothes were predominantly black, accented with berets and cigarette holders; he peppered his speech with foreign words, and had an air about him of European cynicism. Most of Jane's classmates thought of him as amusing at best and arrogant at worst, but Jane was intrigued. She sensed immense talent in him, and saw his airs as protection against vulnerability.

Voutsinas helped Jane bring out the sensitivity in her nature that her upbringing had taught her to repress. Acting—letting one's emotions come rushing to the surface—was alien to everything Jane had experienced since childhood, and Voutsinas urged her to overcome her subconscious reticence about it. He also gave her impeccable advice, and seemed willing to subjugate much of his own ambition to her talent, which he told her he considered the greatest he had ever seen.

Feeling that her rebelliousness was a key to unleashing her talent, Voutsinas encouraged Jane's desire to play against type, to avoid roles that cast her as a proper young society girl. Her own awakening to sexual freedom flew in the face of all she had been taught, and playing sexually loose women was a way to publicly renounce the strictures of her upbringing —and make her own mark in show business. Before long the former tomboy and proper young Vassar girl would become America's newest sex symbol.

Sean Garrison with Jane in her first Broadway play, *There Was a Little Girl,* in which she portrayed a young woman raped by a hoodlum after her sexual advances toward her boyfriend are spurned—and who wonders whether she indeed invited the rape, as her attacker claims. An old friend of Henry's, director Joshua Logan, became aware of Jane through her studies at the Actors Studio, and cast her in a leading role in her first Broadway outing—despite Henry's protestations: "My father thought the play and the part weren't right for me. It was about rape . . . I think he wanted to protect me from what he thought would be a disaster. But I thought, 'Who am I to turn down such a part—the leading role in a Broadway play?' It was a great opportunity. I knew that every young actress in New York would have given her eyeteeth for the part . . . Three days before I accepted [it], my father called me and begged me to turn it down. But I didn't."

Laurence Harvey presents Jane with the *Theater World* Award as "one of the promising personalities of the 1959–1960 season," May 17, 1960. Despite Jane's lofty theatrical ambitions, they would soon take a back seat to her efforts in another entertainment arena—Hollywood.

With Ruth Matteson as her mother in *There Was a Little Girl,* Jane relished the burden she bore playing this important role: "I had had so little responsibility in my life that I loved having demands made on me—to be someplace at a definite hour, with something definite to do. I began to feel a connection with myself. I felt accepted."

There Was a Little Girl opened in New York on February 29, 1960, at the Cort Theater. Although the play was disparaged by the critics and lasted only eighteen performances, Jane's personal notices were excellent. Brooks Atkinson, dean of theater critics, wrote in the New York *Times,* "Although Miss Fonda looks a great deal like her father, her acting style is her own. As the wretched heroine of this unsavory melodrama, she gives an alert, many-sided performance that is professionally mature and suggests that she has found a career that suits her."

Jane's experience with this play convinced her of that. "The Boston critics said I was fragile, when I'm really strong as an ox. They said I was coltish, febrile, virginal, translucent—me! I realized I had created something that moved an audience. From there on I wanted to do nothing else in life but become the greatest stage actress there ever was."

OPPOSITE Jane as college cheerleader June Ryder in her first film, *Tall Story*. After *There Was a Little Girl*, Joshua Logan, who had directed *Picnic, South Pacific,* and *Bus Stop* (guiding Marilyn Monroe therein to her first great performance), saw tremendous potential in Jane, both artistic and commercial. He signed her to a seven-year, seven-film personal contract, paying her ten thousand dollars a year. (Within two years, however, Jane wanted out: Logan was by then being paid hundreds of thousands of dollars for her services and pocketing the difference. She bought back her contract for two hundred fifty thousand dollars, and from then on was a free agent.)

Initially, Logan wanted to costar Jane with Warren Beatty, another screen newcomer. He tested them together, and—although Jane thought she looked as though she had "chipmunk cheeks stuffed with nuts" —Logan was quite impressed with the screen presence of both of them. Warner Bros., however, wanted a more established actor to play opposite Jane in her film debut.

With Anthony Perkins, whom Logan cast as the basketball player who is co-ed Jane's only reason for going to college. A full costarring movie role for Jane at this stage in her career was undoubtedly more a result of her last name than her experience, but she proved herself not only an able actress but a charismatic screen personality as well. According to Perkins, she found it easier to act in front of the movie cameras than the still variety. He recalled a story conference in Logan's apartment at which a studio photographer wanted some publicity shots of the couple necking on the couch. "Jane turned pale. It was her first encounter with one of the absurdities of this business, and it was as if she said to herself, 'My God, is this what being an actress means?' You could see her take a deep breath and say to herself, 'Well, I guess it is, so okay, let's get it over with.'"

Most critics reviled *Tall Story* upon its release in April 1960. *Time*'s review noted, "Nothing could possibly save this picture, not even the painfully personal Perkins doing his famous awkward act, not even a second-generation Fonda with a smile like her father's and legs like a chorus girl." Several critics did single Jane out for praise, however: "The picture wouldn't be reviewed in these pages but for the fact that Henry Fonda's daughter Jane makes her screen debut in it," *Films in Review* said. "She is a good-looking lass and she can act . . . There are a few moments in this picture when in Miss Fonda's eyes it is possible to see the lineaments of her father. Such moments are rare on the screen and rare in film history."

Logan himself admits that the film "was not one of my prouder moments as a screen director . . . nevertheless, I'll always remember it with a bit of fondness for what it represented—Jane's debut. I'll tell you this: with the exception of Marilyn Monroe, I have never worked with a more talented actress than Jane Fonda."

OPPOSITE Jane's own feelings about *Tall Story* were mixed. The filming had not been a pleasant experience for her; she disliked the way she looked on film and was convinced that the movie's crew resented her casting as nepotism. Disillusioned, she returned to New York, and didn't make another film for two years.

Still, the motion-picture debut of Henry Fonda's daughter was greeted with a great deal of fanfare. Hollywood gossip doyenne Louella Parsons devoted a full column to her, anointing Jane with her coveted seal of approval: "Quite a girl, my old friend Hank Fonda's daughter. Beautiful, talented and charming. I invited her to come to see me again soon." Within months of the Parsons column, Jane was featured in *Look* and on the cover of *Life*. Whatever the merits of her first film, Jane Fonda had arrived as the hot new starlet of the day.

Jane with Madeleine Sherwood and a young costar in *Invitation to a March.* The story revolved around a pretty young woman (Jane) who leads such a conventional life that she literally sleeps through most of it. Much of the play's action concerns two women who fight for control of the girl's life, one desiring to keep it as it is, the other feeling she needs more excitement and nonconformity. "The part of Norma Brown was the story of me," Jane said. "A conventional girl, a sleeping beauty who is awakened to love by the kiss of a boy."

OPPOSITE With love interest James MacArthur. Although she was excited about working with such fine actors, Jane was also intimidated; she felt unworthy to be on a Broadway stage with them. "In the beginning," she said, "when I first went on stage, I always felt like apologizing to the audience." At the start of the run, Jane would study the people in the audience before the curtain went up, trying to guess how they would react to her. "If I saw mean faces, I'd feel terrible."

Despite her fears, Jane's reviews when *Invitation to a March* opened on October 29, 1960 were her best so far, and the play ran for three months. Critics called her "the handsomest, smoothest and most delectable ingenue on Broadway" and "the loveliest and most gifted of all our new young actresses." Kenneth Tynan of *The New Yorker* effused, "Jane Fonda can quiver like a tuning fork, and her neurotic outbursts are as shocking as the wanton, piecemeal destruction of a priceless harpsichord. What is more, she has extraordinary physical resources."

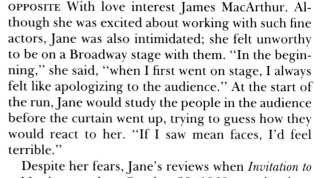

George Grizzard and Jane in a scene from her first television appearance, a color broadcast of W. Somerset Maugham's short story, "A String of Beads," telecast over NBC on February 7, 1961.

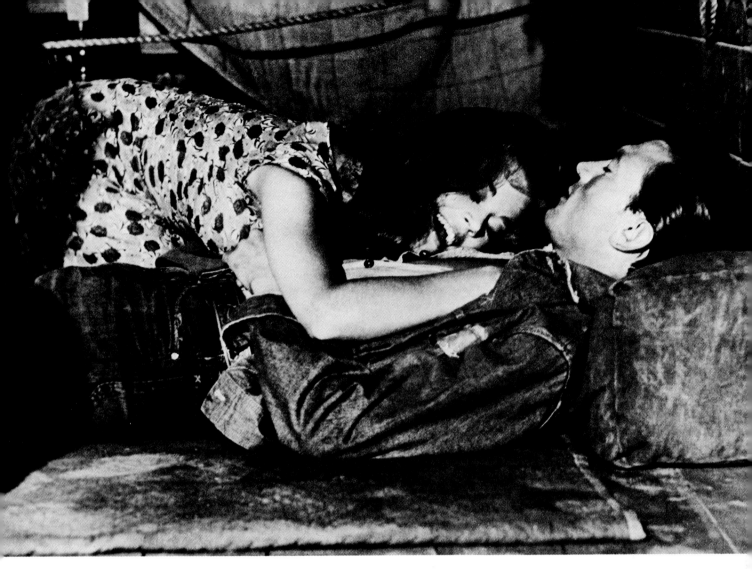

OPPOSITE Jane strikes an appropriately sleazy pose in this scene from *Walk on the Wild Side,* the exploitative screen version of Nelson Algren's novel. The story of a young Texan (Laurence Harvey) who searches for a lost love, only to find her working in a bordello, the film cast Jane as Kitty Twist, a wanton, bratty child-woman also employed by the questionable establishment. Jane was drawn to the part because of her desire to play characters other than goody-goody ingenues, and she worked Kitty Twist's sensuality for all it was worth.

Whether it was her insecurity or a case of her character's personality affecting her own, Jane appears to have been uncharacteristically difficult on this film. Gossip columnist Sidney Skolsky said, "She was always talking loudly about the morons in the picture business. She refused to wear undergarments in scenes after being directed to do so, and went far past the line of duty and good behavior in the fight scene with Sherry O'Neil. Jane bloodied Miss O'Neil's nose . . ."

With Laurence Harvey in one of the film's steamier scenes. There *was* resentment against Jane among the crew on this film, caused chiefly by the presence of Andreas Voutsinas. Having grown increasingly dependent upon him, Jane insisted that he be there to coach her performance every step of the way. This caused friction between Jane and the director, Edward Dmytryk, and things weren't helped by the fact that scarcely anyone connected with Jane or the picture could tolerate Voutsinas. They described him as "imperious," a "creep," "a preening little guy all filled up with his own self-importance," and they couldn't understand Jane's commitment to him. Clearly, though, despite the opposition to Andreas of everyone close to her—including her father—Jane felt a need to have Voutsinas around. "I feel you have to learn as much as you can . . . I don't like the idea of turning people against me, but I've gotten over the feeling that everybody has to love me."

A glamorous publicity pose for the film. Laurence Harvey, for his part, found Jane "easy to get along with, though she seems uncomfortable with touching or displays of affection." She was uneasy, too, about acting sleazy in front of another costar, the veteran actress Barbara Stanwyck, an old friend of the family, who had bounced Jane on her knee when she was a child, and still called her Lady Jane. Called on to act particularly trashy in one scene, Jane froze. "I just couldn't do it in front of Barbara Stanwyck," she later explained. "It was an example of my past confronting my newer self, and in such confrontations, the past usually wins."

Critics thoroughly roasted *Walk on the Wild Side* when it opened in February 1962. Bosley Crowther wrote in the New York *Times,* "Everything in this sluggish picture . . . smacks of sentimentality and social naïveté. It is incredible that anything so foolish would be made in this day and age." Paul Beckley added in the *Herald Tribune,* "The movie has oversimplified and overstated Algren's novel. The characters seem pretentious, overdone . . . Jane Fonda, as a bouncy, wiggly, bratty little thief and prostitute, seems more like a Nelson Algren character than anyone else in the picture." The film was controversial, made money, and further cemented Jane Fonda's reputation as a "hot property."

During rehearsals for *The Fun Couple,* Jane poses with costars (left to right) Ben Piazza, Dyan Cannon, and Bradford Dillman. The play was a very personal project for Jane and Andreas; they saw it as a chance to make Jane a major Broadway star and turn Andreas from an acting coach into a director. Unfortunately, the script—which concerned two young people who marry immediately after meeting each other, and the inevitable problems that follow—wasn't very funny, and the novice playwrights were unable to do the kind of rewrites that Voutsinas quickly saw were the only way to save the show.

Still, he pressed on—because, some say, he was determined to have a Broadway credit to his name at any cost. Jane, completely under his spell, allowed him to make every decision—including choosing her wardrobe. When the play opened on October 26, 1962, it was an unmitigated disaster. Many members of the audience—some of them friends of Jane and Andreas from the Actors Studio—walked out. Critic Walter Kerr wrote: "I find it impossible to believe that *The Fun Couple* ever went out of town. If they'd gone out of town, they'd have closed it." Later, he added, "If you asked me for a list of the five worst plays of all time, *The Fun Couple* would be on it." Luckily for Jane, some attention was diverted from this ignominious failure by her third film, *The Chapman Report,* which had opened in New York eight days earlier.

OPPOSITE Fonda as Kathleen Barclay, the frigid widow in George Cukor's film of Irving Wallace's bestseller *The Chapman Report*. Once again Jane was cast in an exploitation film, this one inspired by the famous Kinsey report on American sexual practices and attitudes. Anxious to work with Cukor—the legendary "women's director" who had guided Greta Garbo, Katharine Hepburn, Jean Harlow, Ingrid Bergman, Joan Crawford, Judy Garland, and Marilyn Monroe, among others—Jane auditioned for the part of a nymphomaniac. Cukor found her audition amusing; he was intrigued by her patrician background and found the possibility of her playing a frigid wife far more interesting. "I was disappointed," Jane said. "But it was George Cukor, and you can wait a lifetime to work with him, so I took the part."

Mrs. Barclay visits Dr. Chapman (Efrem Zimbalist, Jr.), who is conducting research into the sex lives of several women in a small town. When criticism arose over Jane's choice of film projects, she said, "I'm always ready to go out and make a mistake, even though I know I may be criticized. I do it because I'm always thinking my life may be over before I have a chance to do some of these crazy things. For instance, I knew that playing Kitty Twist would make me look very ugly. I thought that my career might be ended because of it, but I went and did it anyway."

Of Cukor, Jane said, "He's a mystical character. He creates women . . . You know he'll protect you. He has impeccable taste and a sense of subtlety. He forces himself to love and believe in you."

Jane made an impression on Cukor as well. "I think the only thing she has to watch is that she has such an abundance of talent she must learn to hold it in. She is an American original."

Things heat up between researcher and subject. *The Chapman Report* met with predictable derision by the critics, who called it a major disappointment from Cukor. It was beginning to look as though Jane's movie career would be checkered at best, and she became an object of ridicule when the *Harvard Lampoon* gave her its "Worst Actress of the Year" award for *The Chapman Report.* But there were those who appreciated Jane in spite of her vehicles, and Stanley Kauffmann, writing in the prestigious *New Republic,* sent Jane a critical valentine: "I have now seen Miss Fonda in three films. In all of them she gives performances that are not only fundamentally different from one another but are conceived without acting cliché and executed with skill. Through them all can be heard, figuratively, the hum of that magnetism without which acting intelligence and technique are admirable but uncompelling . . . It would be unfair to Miss Fonda and the reader to skimp her sex appeal . . . What lies ahead of this appealing and gifted young actress in our theater and film world? Does she stand a chance of fulfillment, or is she condemned—more by our environment than by managers—to mere success? With good parts in good plays and films, she could develop into a first-rate artist. Meanwhile, it would be a pity if her gifts were not fully appreciated in these lesser, though large, roles."

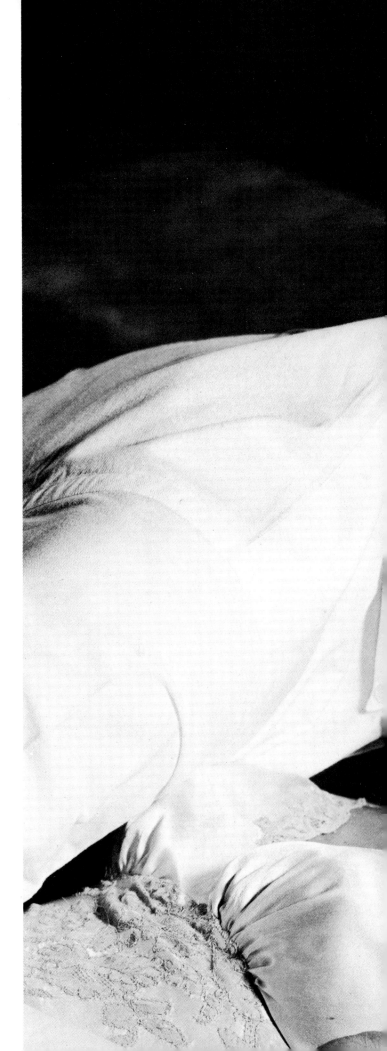

OPPOSITE Jane as Isobel Haverstick, the befuddled newlywed in *Period of Adjustment,* the film version of Tennessee Williams's only comedy. The story of two marriages, one beginning and the other falling apart, appealed to Jane because "it's a story of the lack of communication between male and female—the old idea that a man must show off his masculinity and a girl must be dainty and weak. They're both so busy living in this framework that they go right past each other."

Jane allowed herself to be made over for this role almost entirely into studio head Jack Warner's vision of what a young actress should be: blond, wiggly, big-busted, and false-eyelashed. Her character was ditsy and her publicity presented her as Hollywood's newest blond bombshell. It was an image that would stay

with her for years. Happily, however, she resisted one piece of advice she reportedly received after her first screen test: to have her jaw broken and reset.

ABOVE Jim Hutton, as Isobel's brand-new hubby, gives Jane a tender kiss. Jane was pleased with her role in *Period of Adjustment.* She had been offered the role on Broadway, and read for it. But, "I didn't understand it at all. I'm sure I gave a bad reading . . . I was too young to know what it was all about when I first read the play, but since then I've learned a few things . . . It was an enormous challenge for me, especially because with my two previous films I felt I'd tried but not gotten a good grasp on the characters I was playing."

39

OPPOSITE Jane in one of a series of stills from the movie which the studio described as revealing "the many faceted Jane Fonda." Most critics agreed that that indeed was what she was—her talents as a comedienne were highly praised. Bosley Crowther asked, "Could it be the late Marilyn Monroe that Miss Fonda seems to resemble? She surely won't mind our saying so." Although *Period of Adjustment* was a flimsy film at best, it was a success at the box office and—perhaps most important—it was the first film Jane had done that she came away liking. "I became an actress because I needed love and support from a lot of people," she said. "But at the beginning I never dreamed I'd end up in the movies. A stage career is what I wanted. But somehow making movies gets to you. It's ego-battering and it's much tougher work, because with all the various things involved it's harder to create a performance. When I did *Adjustment* I finally began to feel like an experienced film actress, and I decided movies were for me."

She wasn't, however, finished with Broadway quite yet. On March 12, 1963, she opened in a limited-run revival of Eugene O'Neill's *Strange Interlude,* starring with (left to right) Geoffrey Horne, Franchot Tone, Geraldine Page, Betty Field, William Prince, Richard Thomas, and Ben Gazzara. Jane appeared only at the end of the nine-act play, and her notices weren't thrilling. Howard Taubman's only comment in the *Herald Tribune* was, "Jane Fonda happily contributed her vivacity and beauty to the final two acts." It was, in fact, working with Geraldine Page that made Jane give up on the theater; Page's brilliance made Jane feel so inadequate on stage that her dreams of achieving theatrical immortality began to seem rather unrealistic.

41

Fonda strikes a highly sophisticated pose in one of her "lost" films, *In the Cool of the Day.* Filmed in Greece, the movie told the story of terminally ill Christine Bonner and her whirlwind love affair while on vacation. Jane and Andreas flew to Paris for a vacation of their own before their trip to Andreas's homeland; but as they were preparing to leave they were informed that since Voutsinas had never served in the Greek Army, he would be drafted immediately upon entering the country. Jane made the trip alone.

OPPOSITE Jane and costar Peter Finch have a little fun during a rehearsal. Laughs were hard to come by for Jane while making this picture. She felt adrift without Voutsinas at a time when she sorely needed him. She realized early on that the script, and Robert Stevens's direction, left a lot to be desired, and she feared that she was mired in a movie that was a sure box-office bomb. She was right.

When the company went to London for several scenes, Andreas was able to rejoin Jane, and he was constantly at her side, guiding, cajoling, and advising her.

Although Jane felt that her association with Andreas had brought her great professional rewards, it tried her already strained relationship with her father. Henry thought Voutsinas was an unwholesome influence on Jane, and he resented the fact that in many ways Andreas had supplanted him as a father figure. Referring to Andreas, Henry said, "I couldn't talk enough about Jane and the good things she has. But in one area she has a blind spot . . . she's going to get hurt." Henry reportedly felt that Andreas was trying to control Jane. "I can't be that much of a Svengali, I really can't, you know," Voutsinas said. "And I'm hurt, very hurt by Jane's father's rejection of me. And so is Jane."

Unable, as usual, to discuss the matter with her father, Jane withdrew further from him and relied even more on Andreas.

Aboard a ferryboat during filming, Jane practices a Greek national folk dance she was required to perform in the movie. Jane took to the new dance form quickly—since childhood she had been an accomplished ballet dancer.

OPPOSITE Christine's lover comforts her as she succumbs to tuberculosis. When *In the Cool of the Day* opened in May of 1963, the reviews were dreadful. Even her erstwhile champion, Stanley Kauffmann, was displeased, although he didn't place the blame on Jane: "If such matters were legally actionable," he wrote in *The New Republic*, "Jane Fonda would have grounds for suit against the director Robert Stevens, the screenwriter Meade Roberts, the cinematographer Peter Newbrook and the wardrobe designer Orry-Kelly, each of whom has put her at a disadvantage in her new film . . . one sees her struggling intelligently to give life to the lumber, and one also sees her consistently defeated. None of these matters handicap Peter Finch, her lover, who is safely asleep throughout."

Luckily for Jane, *In the Cool of the Day* opened and closed almost immediately, and few people saw it.

OPPOSITE September 1963: Jane poses prettily as her hair is done in her Paris hotel room. In France to star in a new film, *Joy House,* for René Clément, she quickly captured the imagination of the French public. They found her coltish grace endearingly American, and her sex appeal international; she was quickly labeled "La BB Americaine," an enormous compliment, since Brigitte Bardot had been the personification of beauty and sensuality in her native country for years. Jane charmed them with her personality as well; she spoke French whenever possible, sometimes fracturing the language and addressing everyone in a formal style roughly translated as "thou." She was compared to a colt in a popular song, and appeared on the cover of dozens of magazines. Press accounts of her appeal bordered on the rhapsodic:

"Tall, blonde, the perfect American, with long, flexible movements," writer Georges Belmont described her. "Inside she is sultry and dangerous, like a caged animal . . . I watched her move and thought in a flash of the black panther I used to watch in the zoo."

"It was wonderful," Jane said of her reception from the French. "I never felt so good."

ABOVE Rod Taylor and Jane in her next film, *Sunday in New York.* Based on the Broadway play which had starred Robert Redford and Pat Stanley (Jane had turned down the stage role), the film was a thin will-she-or-won't-she sex comedy, which also starred Cliff Robertson and Robert Culp.

47

OPPOSITE Jane checks her makeup during a break in filming. She thoroughly enjoyed the production of this picture, and it further strengthened her commitment to films: "Making the picture was completely fun from start to finish," she said, "which is more than I can say for the other films I've made. The part could have been boring, but it wasn't. I'm sure this movie will help my career."

ABOVE During filming on the streets of New York, Henry and Peter visit Jane, both carrying the scripts of *their* current projects: Henry's *Fail Safe* and Peter's *Lilith*.

Despite such public displays of family harmony, Henry Fonda was estranged from both his children, and Jane had begun to air publicly her misgivings about her father. She disclosed during one interview that she was undergoing analysis, and intimated that her early life was one of the things that had sent her into therapy. She added, "Daddy should have been analyzed forty years ago."

Henry was hurt and defensive about his daughter's lack of discretion. "I'm between planes somewhere, and before long there's a reporter to interview me, and he has a clipping that says Jane Fonda thinks her parents led a phony life. Or that she thinks her father should have been psychoanalyzed . . . now it's all

right for her to think it, but I don't think it's all right for her to say so in interviews. After all, I *am* her father. I mean, that's disrespectful. And some of the things she's been saying—well, they just aren't true."

The lack of communication and understanding between Jane and Henry became painfully obvious during another "interview exchange" between them. Jane told a reporter, "I used to come home from [Lee Strasberg's] classes so full of what I was doing, and my father would say, 'Shut up, I don't want to hear about it.' There was one time, for example, when I had just done a marvelous scene in class . . . I wanted to tell him about it. And I could see his curtain come down. He smiled, but I just didn't get through."

Told of Jane's comment, Henry said, "Well, I don't understand this . . . maybe I do things that I'm not aware of that mean something to other people. I don't know what she means by a curtain coming down." He then related a story of feeling particularly proud of Jane, but "I wasn't going to let her see me go on like this." When the interviewer, Alfred Aronowitz, asked him why not, and said that she wanted to reach her father, Fonda said, "Well, gosh, she does get to me."

"She wants to *know* she's getting to you," Aronowitz said. "She's such a demonstrative person."

"Well," Fonda said in conclusion, "I'm not."

OPPOSITE Fonda, Taylor, and costars prepare a scene on location in Manhattan. Jane was right—*Sunday in New York* did help her career. Although the film was criticized for its sexual coyness, the public loved it, and it became Jane's first bonafide box-office hit. And her character—an attractive, stylish, principled young woman—was closer to the way the public wanted to think of Jane than the sexual aberrants she had played in several of her earlier films. By now, Jane Fonda was considered a major Hollywood star, and reviewers were discussing the bright prospects of her acting future with increasing regularity. *Motion Picture* magazine: "Now that she has mastered this role, it is time for her to move on to more challenging stuff. Unlike most of her costars, she has the raw material to develop, if she's willing to give it a try."

For a *Paris-Match* photo layout, Jane dresses as a turn-of-the-century man of leisure, looking, as the caption pointed out, like "an anemic Charlie Chaplin." Other scenes created for the whimsical Belle Époque spread were the end of a romance, an evening in a glamorous restaurant, a bedroom farce and a waltz.

OPPOSITE In the summer of 1964, Jane purchased her first home—a 130-year-old farm in the French countryside, about eighty kilometers from Paris. The picturesque but dilapidated property—on three acres of land—completely charmed Jane and she set about renovating it with zeal. She gutted the inside and supervised its modernization, pitching in to do whatever work she could. She also redid the grounds: "The land was flat, and there weren't any trees, so I had a bulldozer come in to move the earth around and give it a more rolling effect, and I had dozens of full-grown trees brought out from Paris and planted. It was wild—every morning you could see these lines of trees advancing up the road like Birnam Wood coming to Dunsinane."

Once her new home was completed, Jane felt more rooted than she had since the days with her family at Tigertail. By settling in France, Jane was putting into motion a series of events which would radically alter her life.

As Melinda in René Clément's film *Les Felins*, entitled *Joy House* in America. The film, intended as a thriller in the Hitchcock tradition, had an almost indescribable plot concerning a petty gangster (Alain Delon) on the run from cohorts he has double-crossed. He meets Jane and Lola Albright at a soup kitchen where they work. The women move Delon into Albright's gothic mansion, where Jane sleeps in his bed, waiting for him to come back from Albright's. He begins to feel threatened by Albright's mad lover, several attempts to poison him—and the shrunken head Albright keeps in a jar. It was all quite absurd, and Jane knew early on that she was making a turkey. "There was no script and very little organization," she said when filming ended. "It sort of threw me because I'm used to working within a structured framework. There was just too much playing it by ear for my taste."

"I will undoubtedly fall in love with Delon," Jane announced to the French press as *Joy House* filming commenced. "I can only play love scenes well when I am in love with my partner."

Although the quote was nine-tenths press agentry, it wasn't long before it proved prophetic. Jane and Delon, seen here vacationing on the French Riviera, began a romance that further intensified the French press's preoccupation with Jane—especially when Delon's romance with Romy Schneider ended publicly to make room for Jane. Delon was one of France's most celebrated male sex symbols, and his reputation as a Lothario, as well as his reputed underworld associations, made him excellent fodder for gossip sheets.

Jane, although captivated by Delon's obvious attributes, began to find him rather dull and less than her intellectual equal, and the relationship petered out. By then, however, Andreas Voutsinas had left France in a huff, never to reenter Jane's life romantically.

OPPOSITE *Joy House* was a moderate success in France, primarily as a result of the storm of publicity surrounding the film. In America, however, it was a commercial and critical bomb. Judith Crist wrote, "Miss Fonda has some mysterious hold over Miss Albright. It's not all Miss Fonda has—or at least so she attempts to indicate by alternatingly impersonating the Madwoman of Chaillot, Baby Doll and her father Henry; she's a sick kid, this one." Stanley Kauffmann added, "The question of Jane Fonda's development into an extraordinarily good actress, which I still think quite possible, is beclouded by her poor choice of vehicles."

Reviews in France were somewhat better. The critic for the magazine *Samedi et Dimanche* wrote, "The major revelation is Jane Fonda, 'the American BB,' as Melinda. Her French is surprisingly good and her sex appeal is estimable. She has the potential to be a sex symbol in the tradition of Bardot or Monroe, and if she collaborates with Vadim, the results will be interesting."

Before long, Jane *did* collaborate with Vadim—personally as well as professionally—and the results were very interesting indeed.

PART THREE

MME. VADIM
1965-68

Jane and Roger Vadim at their Malibu, California,
home in 1965.

Jane Fonda first met Roger Vadim in the fall of 1957, during her initial stay in Paris. Vadim's controversial—some would say scandalous—first film, *And God Created Woman*, had just been released, and it became a *cause célèbre* on two continents. The film, which starred his wife, Brigitte Bardot, presented a much more blatant sexuality than had ever been allowed on screen before. Vadim's personal life had a hint of *le scandale* about it as well: he had moved into Bardot's parents' home when she was sixteen, waited until she was of age, then married and molded her from a shy brunette into an undulating blond sex kitten—and the most famous bombshell since Monroe.

Vadim, it has been said, eyed Fonda with great interest during that first encounter at Maxim's, despite the fact that he was with his second wife, Annette Stroyberg, who had given birth to his child the day after his divorce from Bardot was final. Jane was wary, and avoided his attentions. "I heard things about him then that would curl your hair. That he was sadistic, vicious, cynical, perverted, that he was a manipulator of women, et cetera . . ."

By the time Jane met him a second time, he had made a star of Stroyberg by directing her in *Les Liaisons Dangereuses,* in which she appeared in the nude; the film was held up two years by censorship problems. Vadim's reputation as an erotic Svengali was further enhanced by his next affair, with eighteen-year-old Catherine Deneuve, another beautiful blonde who bore him a child out of wedlock.

When Jane met Vadim again in the early sixties, she had even more reason to be wary of him. He had requested a meeting to discuss doing a film with her. "I went, but I was terrified," she said. "Like I thought he was going to rape me right there in the Polo Lounge. But he was terribly quiet and polite. I thought, 'Boy, what a clever act.'" Jane had her agents wire regrets.

While she was in Paris to film *La Curée,* Jane had become as much a media darling as Vadim, and now she was more nearly his equal, both in her professional stature and her maturity. She didn't hesitate when he requested they get together again to discuss a possible film collaboration. This time, Jane was able to see through Vadim's public image. "I'm older, and I think, 'Christ, I never gave the guy a chance.' Well, I was floored. He was the antithesis of what I'd been told. I found a shyness . . ."

For Vadim, this new, sophisticated, self-possessed young lady was even more intriguing than she had been six years earlier. He was, in fact—as the French say—"hit by lightning": "For the second time in my life, I was to be the victim of that strange disease, love at first sight."

It took longer for Jane; she agreed to star in Vadim's *La Ronde,* and it was during filming that she fell in love. "I discovered a very gentle man. So many men in America are . . . men-men, always having to prove their strength and masculinity. Vadim was not afraid to be vulnerable—even feminine, in a way. And I was terrified of being vulnerable."

Jane had a greater need than ever to throw off the inhibitions that had been ingrained in her. She felt emotionally repressed, sexually unliberated, intellectually conventional. Vadim's mind, his sexual and social unconventionality, his circle of friends, all appealed to Jane's ever-growing rebelliousness. She accepted Vadim's sexual code as her own: "I told Jane that I am incapable of making love to one woman all my life. 'If I have a sex adventure,' I said, 'I will not lie to you. But one thing I promise you—it will not be important. I could not have a mistress. Also I will not behave in public in such a way as to embarrass you, because it will not be an elegance to you.'"

That so worldly a man had such respect for her deeply impressed Jane. He had an uncommon understanding of women in general and Jane in particular, and he was better able to help Jane understand herself than anyone she had ever known. As Vadim put it, "Like all the women I have been involved with, she had a . . . vulnerability. Nothing is more attractive than vulnerability in a woman. She wants to be beautiful but is not sure that she is. She wants to be happy but manages always to be unhappy. Jane always thought that to be happy you must build walls to protect yourself from unhappiness. If I taught her anything it was to be more herself, not to be afraid . . . you ask if the walls were high? They were a fortress! The Great Wall of China!"

Jane's relationship with Roger Vadim proved profoundly important in her life. He orchestrated her career over the next six years, brought out her genuine sensuality and sexuality as no one before him had done, and created her in the public mind as a sexual icon. Privately, Vadim's attempts to make her "more herself" and "not afraid" would result in an astonishing turnabout in Jane Fonda's personality—one that would change Jane's fundamental perceptions, alter the public's perception of her—and, ironically, ultimately destroy the Vadim marriage.

OPPOSITE A pouty Jane shares a scene with costar Maurice Ronet in Roger Vadim's film *La Ronde (Circle of Love).* It had been said of Vadim that he had a habit of turning his paramours into replicas of Brigitte Bardot, and it certainly seemed true of Jane in this film: she was softer, prettier, and more sensual than she had ever been before.

Circle of Love was a remake of a classic 1954 French film starring the revered Danielle Darrieux in the Fonda role of an unfaithful wife. The new version broke little new ground; its plot also revolved around a woman who bedhopped between her husband and lover. The atmosphere on the set was sexually charged, what with Jane in bed most of the time, but she denied rumors in the French press that she was acting in the nude. "I am supposedly nude in bed," she retorted, "but I wear a bra and panties. There were ninety-five people on the set and I'd be embarrassed . . ."

According to some of those ninety-five people, Jane was less embarrassed by the constant coaching Vadim was giving her in the proper way to make love on screen; it quickly became clear to all that Jane and Vadim were more than just actress and director.

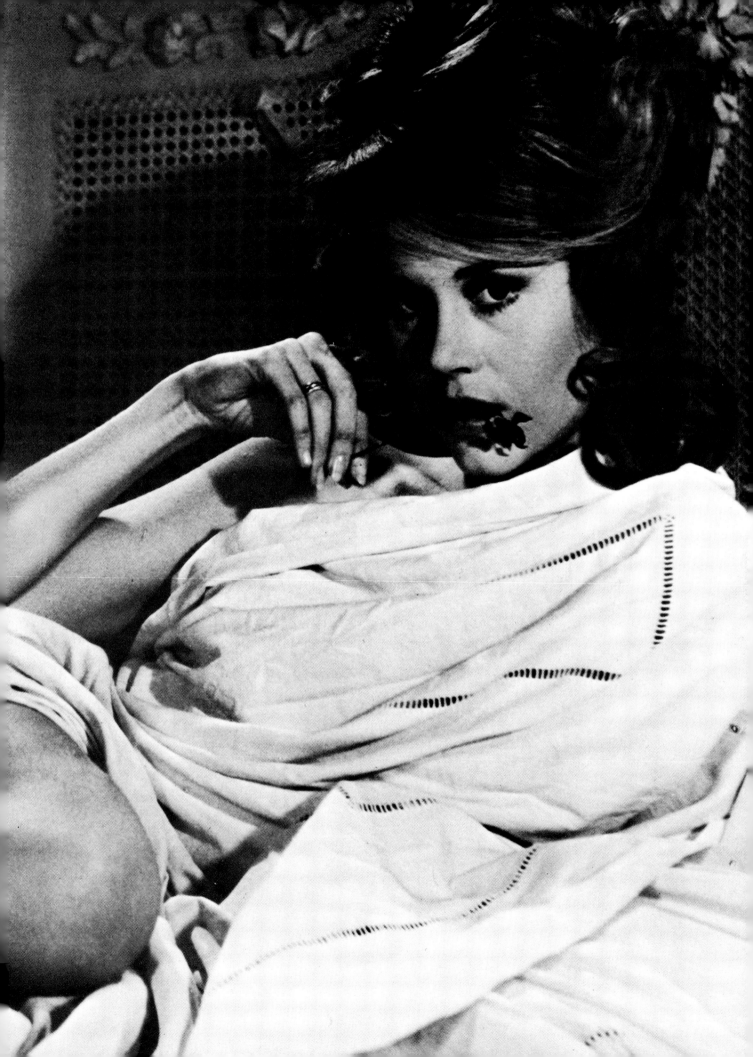

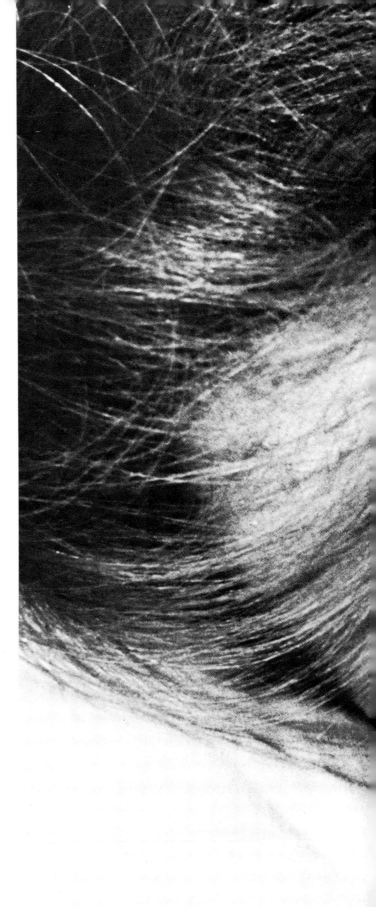

Circle of Love was a moderate success, and once again Jane's reviews were good, although she was frequently compared unfavorably to Danielle Darrieux: "Wildly miscast as the discreet and timid matron, the part Miss Darrieux made hers for life, the improving Miss Fonda plays against type," wrote Eugene Archer in the New York *Times*. "With some comic skill, she creates a perverse imp who speaks modestly while her gestures and expressions pointedly belie her words." *Samedi et Dimanche* added, "Jane Fonda . . . may be the next actress Vadim molds into a child-woman of universal appeal . . . He has never before had the opportunity to mold an American, and only time will tell whether this seemingly emancipated woman bends to his will. Fonda's range is greater than earlier Vadim creations, and she would probably have had a flourishing career even if she had not been born the daughter of Henry Fonda and even if she had never set foot in France."

The Great Jane Fonda Billboard Cover-up. As *Circle of Love* was about to open at the DeMille Theater near Broadway, a billboard eight stories high appeared in front of the theater, with a naked Jane reclining in bed, her derrière in plain view. Several New York newspaper columnists expressed shock and outrage, and Jane was mortified. She filed a three-million-dollar lawsuit against the theater's owners, who covered up the offending portion of the billboard with canvas, thereby drawing more attention to it and winning even more publicity for the film. Eventually, the billboard was taken down and Jane dropped the lawsuit.

OPPOSITE January 1965: Jane is the height of mid-sixties fashion as she makes an appearance in London to promote *La Ronde*.

OPPOSITE The satiric Western *Cat Ballou* cast Jane as the sweetly innocent schoolteacher Catherine Ballou, who becomes a dangerous gunslinger to avenge her father's murder; reacts to the sheriff's corruption by heading up a gang of outlaws; accidentally kills her father's murderer; and is rescued from the gallows by her followers.

ABOVE With Lee Marvin as Kid Shelleen, the besotted gunfighter who helps Cat find her father's killers, a gang led by the deliciously evil Jim Strawn (also played by Marvin), who sports a silver nose to replace his own, which was bitten off in a fight.

Cat Ballou was a marvelous send-up of every conceivable Western cliché; Jane's performance sparkled, and Lee Marvin's hilarious depictions of both characters won him the Oscar as the Best Actor of 1965 and elevated him from character villain to star. Director Elliot Silverstein credits Jane with creating the framework for Marvin's accomplishment: "He played off a foundation that she supplied. She was a workhorse. It's hard to supply the means by which others have all the fun . . . She had to hold it all together, which she did without any question."

OPPOSITE Costar Michael Callan gives Jane a kiss in one of *Cat Ballou*'s rare quiet moments. The film became a huge commercial success, and it was easy to see during filming that it was going to be a hit. Jane's confidence and good humor translated beautifully into her performance—and the fact that her beloved Vadim was on the set with her helped considerably.

Like Jane, her coworkers had heard the most disturbing things about Vadim, and they were surprised to find him accessible as well as eccentric. As one of the actors put it: "Here was this Frenchman in horn-rimmed glasses reading *Mad* magazine—all by himself, sitting on a camp chair on the mountainside while Jane was filming. They weren't standoffish at all. Between scenes, at lunch, they joked around with everyone. Vadim's a very friendly guy."

A moody portrait of Jane on the set of *Cat Ballou*. The film raised Jane's stock in Hollywood considerably, and although her presence could not be said to be the sole reason for its financial success, her performance was widely acknowledged as a major reason the parody worked so well. As *Time* put it, "In a performance that nails down her reputation as a girl worth singing about, actress Fonda does every preposterous thing demanded of her with a giddy sincerity that is at once beguiling, poignant and hilarious. Wearing widow's weeds over her six-guns, she romps through one of the zaniest train robberies ever filmed, a throwback to Pearl White's perilous heyday. Putting the final touches on a virginal white frock to wear at her own hanging, she somehow suggests that Alice in Wonderland has fallen among blackguards and rather enjoys it. Happily, *Cat Ballou* makes the enjoyment epidemic."

On August 15, 1965, Mr. and Mrs. Roger Vadim admire her wedding ring the day after their marriage in Las Vegas, Nevada. Vadim had been urging Jane to marry him for some time, but she resisted, still feeling—as she had stated earlier—that marriage was obsolete. Asked why she changed her mind, she replied, "Well, I guess because of my father. I knew I was hurting him." Henry had harbored doubts about Vadim, although far fewer than he had about Voutsinas. An earlier visit to the couple's home on the beach at Malibu may not have made him feel better that they were living together without benefit of matrimony, but it did put his mind at ease about their life-style. Jane explained, "One day the phone rang, and it was Dad saying he wanted to come over. He had never met Vadim, and he wanted to dislike him. He came into our house expecting God knows what after all the things he had heard, an orgy, I suppose. But there I was slopping around in blue jeans and Vadim was sitting on the deck fishing, one of Father's passions in life."

Jane as Anna Reeves, wife of an escaped convict, in Arthur Penn's film *The Chase.* Jane had lobbied for the role, because few films—on paper—had more potential for artistic and commercial success than this one. Its producer was Sam Spiegel, whose films *On The Waterfront, Bridge on the River Kwai* and *Suddenly, Last Summer* were classics; its director was Arthur Penn, who, although a newcomer, had already won high praise for *The Miracle Worker* and *Mickey One;* its screenwriter was Lillian Hellman; and its other stars—Marlon Brando, Robert Redford, James Fox, and Angie Dickinson—were all not only extraordinarily talented but charismatic as well.

OPPOSITE On the set with Robert Redford, who played Anna's husband, Bubber, whose escape from jail precipitates the film's action and fires up the passions of an entire town: Anna is having an affair with the son (James Fox) of the town's powerful and manipulative oil baron (E. G. Marshall), who for his own reasons doesn't want Bubber back in the town. The townspeople, fired up into a drunken, bigoted frenzy against Bubber, form a lynch mob as the principled sheriff (Brando)—who believes Bubber innocent of the murder charges that imprisoned him—tries to bring Bubber in alive. On the steps of the jailhouse, a local goon shoots and kills Bubber.

On the last day of filming, Redford, Fonda, and James Fox celebrate with abandon. Jane was undoubtedly happy to have this picture finished, because by then she was aware that—despite all its promise—it was not going to be good. The final product, released in February 1966, was an overblown, heavy-handed melodrama roasted by the critics and disliked by audiences; at the end of one screening people booed and jeered. *Time*'s critic wrote: *"The Chase* is a shockworn message film, smoothly overacted and topheavy with subtle bigotry, expertly exploiting the violence, intolerance and mean provincialism that it is supposed to be preaching against . . . Miss Hellman seldom lets a scene end without tacking on her comment; except for a handful of courageous, long-suffering Negroes and Sheriff Brando, no Texan escapes being singed by a Statement . . . Jane Fonda conquers a casting error as Bubber's faithless wife, making trollopy white trash seem altogether first class."

No one seemed willing to take the blame for the failure of *The Chase.* Spiegel and Penn accused the front office of Columbia Pictures of pressuring them into hoking up the film; Hellman blamed Spiegel, Penn, and two other writers she said were responsible for script changes that ruined the film: "What was intended as a modest picture about some aimless people on an aimless Saturday night got hot and large . . ." For her part, Jane Fonda has reserved comment.

75

OPPOSITE Jane's next film—her tenth—wasn't a much happier experience. *Any Wednesday* was based on a surprisingly successful Broadway bedroom farce by Muriel Resnick. Jane played Ellen Gordon, the thirty-year-old mistress of a corporate bigwig who longs for the legitimacy of marriage and takes a lover, complicating her comfortable setup.

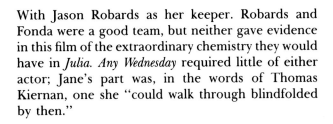

With Jason Robards as her keeper. Robards and Fonda were a good team, but neither gave evidence in this film of the extraordinary chemistry they would have in *Julia*. *Any Wednesday* required little of either actor; Jane's part was, in the words of Thomas Kiernan, one she "could walk through blindfolded by then."

Ellen laments her plight to her new boyfriend, played by Dean Jones. *Any Wednesday* wasn't a disaster, but neither was it much of a success. While some reviews were kind to Jane and the film, Rex Reed's patented vitriol came closer to the consensus: "*Any Wednesday* is a good example of the movies taking everything that is crisp and human about the stage and turning it into everything that is loud and vulgar and boring about Hollywood. Simply everything is wrong with this loudmouthed movie . . . The story of a 30-year-old mistress who never grew up (played with strokes of cotton-candy brilliance and big feet by Sandy Dennis onstage) gets all but stomped on with cleated boots by Jane Fonda. She is about as funny as a manic-depressive having her first nervous breakdown. She screams, weeps, beats the furniture, picks at her cuticles, and when she has no lines she just pouts and fusses with her fright wig."

Peter McEnery and Jane in Vadim's *The Game Is Over*, his version of Émile Zola's classic novel *La Curée*. Jane played a pampered French wife who falls in love with her stepson (McEnery), who is about her own age. Most of the film revolves around their idyllic love affair, with beautifully photographed romantic interludes.

OPPOSITE For the first time, Jane appeared fully nude in this motion picture; despite her prior claims that she would never do so, Vadim convinced her of the necessity of nudity in the creation of this character. It was to cause her extreme embarrassment, however: without her knowledge, a still photographer recorded a nude swimming scene, revealing all of Jane, even though in the film she is seen only from the back. When Jane heard that *Playboy* intended to publish the pictures, she threatened legal action, but the magazine proceeded. Jane was furious, and her multimillion-dollar lawsuit claimed that her nudity in the film was her fictional character's, not her own, and that the photographs as published invaded her privacy. Jane eventually lost the suit—and was not happy about reports that Vadim had been aware of the photographer's presence all along.

The Game Is Over proved to be intelligent and sensitive, and Vadim elicited from his wife what many consider her first great dramatic performance. The film, released in January 1967, was a smash hit in Europe—it's considered a minor classic there—and was helped to respectable grosses in the United States by reviews like Kevin Thomas's in the Los Angeles *Times:* "Roger Vadim's films are visual memoirs of his amours. He has made love with a camera to former wives Brigitte Bardot and Annette Stroyberg, who glowed on the screen in response. But he has never made it so well as with Jane Fonda, the current Mme. Vadim, who is not only as gorgeous as her predecessors but also a gifted actress . . . Having trusted Vadim completely, she creates a comprehensive portrait of a woman in love—her joys and sorrows, hopes and fears."

OPPOSITE Jane gives Michael Caine an appropriately disgusted look as he—playing her alcoholic husband —paws her in Otto Preminger's sordid Southern melodrama *Hurry Sundown*. After the fiasco of *The Chase,* Jane apparently felt Preminger might have a better chance at creating an important picture about the tragedy of bigotry: "(He's) one of the rare ones who can be a showman and an artist at the same time." Jane once again played a wanton woman, this one so frustrated by her husband's booze-induced impotence that she takes his saxophone, puts it between his legs and blows on it with slow and highly suggestive determination.

In addition to sex, *Hurry Sundown* featured racial hatred, corruption, land theft, arson, dynamitings and near lynchings.

ABOVE Jane and costars Diahann Carroll and Faye Dunaway enjoy a rare light moment during filming. As melodramatic as *Hurry Sundown* turned out, the fact that art in this case was simply imitating life hit home quickly with the cast and crew. The presence of Carroll and another black, Robert Hooks, at the Louisiana location created several unpleasant scenes. As Jane has recalled, "We had this swimming pool at the motel and I'll never forget the first day one of the Negro actors jumped in. There were reverberations all the way to New Orleans. People just stood and stared like they expected the water to turn black."

Things grew ugly when the Ku Klux Klan "ordered" Preminger to put "the niggers" in a separate all-black hotel. He refused, with the backing of Jane and all the other members of the company. Things came to a head one afternoon shortly thereafter. As Jane was walking down a street, a little black boy ran up to her with a flower. Grateful, she bent down and kissed him. As Vadim remembers, "People stopped and stared at us in silence. The atmosphere in the street, which only a moment before had been gay and full of life, became heavy and uncomfortable and vaguely threatening."

A short while later, the local sheriff ordered the entire company out of town "for their own safety"— the Ku Klux Klan was threatening to kill Preminger. He was given a half hour to get his people out of town, and as they left, bullets shattered two of their windshields.

With Diahann Carroll, whose face she has just slapped for being in a "Whites Only" ladies' room. *Hurry Sundown* was savaged by reviewers when it opened in March 1967, both for its heavy-handed examples of racism and skulduggery and for its clichéd, trite relationships. Critics ridiculed the dialogue and turned positively purple over Jane's saxophone scene. Words used to describe the film included "offensive," "ludicrous," and "tasteless." Judith Crist wrote, "Preminger has provided us not only with soap opera plotting that gives *Peyton Place* Dostoievskian stature but also with cartoon characters and patronage of Negroes that are incredible in 1967." Rex Reed, after offering a vivid description of the saxophone scene ("She jes' falls between his knees and puts the butt of his saxophone right in her mouth with the slobber fallin' down her chin and all . . .") added, "At the screening I attended, the audience was hissing and booing and throwing popcorn boxes at the screen with such nasty vigor I almost missed the scene where the judge spit into the church communion cup. Unfortunately, they quieted down long enough for me to hear Jane Fonda gurgle, 'I was ten years old before I learned *damn* and *Yankee* were two different words.' "

Fortunately for Jane, one of her biggest successes was ready for release just two months after *Hurry Sundown.*

The Roger Vadims are remarried on May 18, 1967, after discovering that their Las Vegas marriage was invalid in France. In their nearly two years of marriage, Vadim had brought out several conflicting characteristics in Jane. She was now an ultrasophisticated, Continental woman at ease with her own sexuality—and at the same time a happily domesticated wife to Vadim, cooking, caring for and deferring to him. Although his worldly views and more radical friends would, ultimately, profoundly alter Jane's perceptions of things, at this point she was perfectly content to be subservient to him—probably because he inspired rather than demanded it.

Robert Redford and Jane as newlyweds Paul and Corie Bratter in Neil Simon's *Barefoot in the Park,* the third Jane Fonda film released in the first five months of 1967. Based on the enormously successful Broadway play (which also starred Redford), the film was a funny, bubbly romp in which Fonda, as a free-spirited whirlwind, tries to loosen up her stuffed-shirt new husband, with predictably zany results.

OPPOSITE Jane camps it up for a publicity still. *Barefoot in the Park* filming may have been the most uneventful of Fonda's career. She got along well with Redford, who had been a friend of hers since *The Chase* ("We share the same causes, Bob and I"), as well as director Gene Saks and costars Mildred Natwick and Charles Boyer (as her mother and a lecherous upstairs neighbor). Boyer commented on Jane: "She speaks very passable French, but she is American through and through. She has an eagerness to learn and do her role as well as she can. I don't always see that in established actresses. I understand her work for Vadim has been very sensual, but she seems very much at home in comedy, and there is a strong sexual undercurrent between her and Redford. They are almost too attractive a pair . . . Jane is a friendly girl, though she does not laugh often and keeps a distance between herself and strangers. But she is compassionate, and she is concerned about more things than her hair . . ."

Barefoot in the Park became Jane's biggest box-office success, and its reviews were generally ecstatic. "Jane's performance," noted *Time*, "is the best of her career; a clever caricature of a sex kitten who can purr or scratch with equal intensity."

The dichotomy that Roger Vadim had brought out in Jane was commented on by Gerald Jonas in the New York *Times:* "Jane Fonda has managed to maintain two entirely different public images simultaneously between France and the United States. Over here she appears in movies like *Barefoot in the Park* and *Any Wednesday;* she sounds and dresses like the pretty roommate of the girl you dated in college, and most people still think of her as Henry Fonda's daughter. Over there she stars in movies like *Circle of Love* and *The Game Is Over.* She sounds like the girl you eavesdropped on in a Paris cafe; she undresses like Brigitte Bardot, and everyone knows her as the latest wife . . . of Roger Vadim."

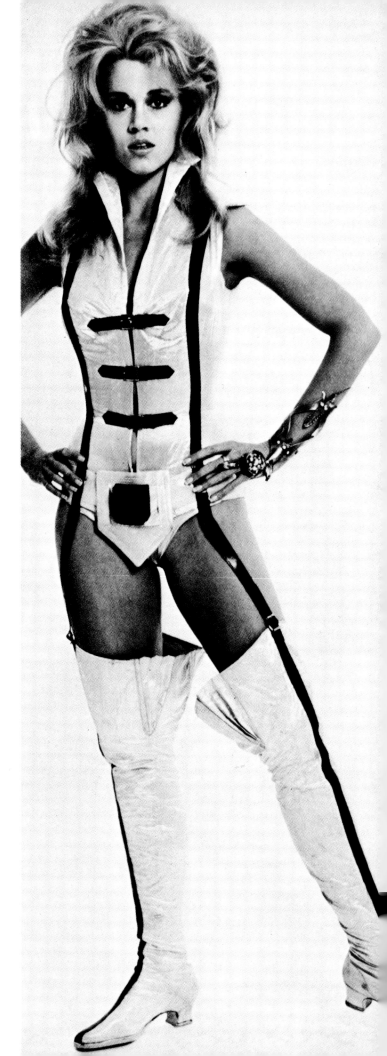

OPPOSITE October 8, 1968, Jane leaves the hospital carrying her daughter, Vanessa, born September 28. A case of mumps had made Jane fearful that her baby would be born damaged, but the child was perfectly healthy. Brigitte Bardot, who had remained close to her ex-husband and befriended Jane, had predicted that the baby would be a girl and be born on Bardot's birthday. Even before BB's predictions came true, Jane asserts, she had visions of the child being a tiny replica of Brigitte.

When Jane began labor, Vadim packed her into their car and started out for the hospital. "Fifty meters from the hospital," Vadim has said, "the automobile stopped. Yes, I had remembered everything except to buy the gas. So I picked up Jane and carried her to the hospital—believe me, it was very dramatic —and one hour later she gave birth."

Jane reveled in her new status as a mother. "It's made my life completely different," she said. "I can't get over the miracle of giving birth. I feel fulfilled, rounder. Little things that used to bother me seem so unimportant now. I want more children. I miss being pregnant. I've never been so elated. The pleasure and pain were so extraordinary that I try to hang on to every memory of them."

Jane as Barbarella, Queen of the Galaxy, in Vadim's film of the popular, sexy French comic strip by Jean-Claude Forest. Long before films based on comic-book heroes became fashionable, Vadim wanted to bring the irreverent, adult-themed *Barbarella* story to the screen. Jane agreed, even though she had begun to express distaste for the sex-kitten aspects of her public image. She said, "The overemphasis on identifying me with sex is pretty silly. I'm no sex siren just because I believe in approaching sex and the human body with honesty . . . I think the whole obsession with sex, and with the size of a girl's breasts, is a perversion—it's a sad comment on the state of manhood in America. The real homosexuals are the big tough guys who think they're so manly. All they're doing is hiding behind their fears. They all want to go back to their mothers' breasts, that's all. If you ask me, the whole business about sex is sickness because it's dishonest."

Ironically, *Barbarella* would establish Jane in the public mind for a long time to come as the archetypal sexpot, and the film would become a cult favorite with many of the men Jane seems to have looked upon with disfavor.

OPPOSITE Barbarella pets one of the strange creatures that inhabit her world in the year 40,000 A.D. With Dino De Laurentiis producing, *Barbarella* had a huge budget, allowing Vadim to create wonderful futuristic sets to contain the far-out happenings surrounding Barbarella's galactic journey in search of the elusive Duran Duran.

ABOVE With John Phillip Law as the Blind Angel and Anita Pallenberg as Barbarella's adversary. Filming *Barbarella* was fraught with difficulty for Jane. The elaborate futuristic gadgets frequently malfunctioned, sometimes with dangerous results. One scene in particular caused Jane extreme distress: Barbarella was to be attacked by two thousand wrens that pick at her clothes until they fall from her body in tatters. The logistics of filming the scene were almost impossible; the birds wouldn't cooperate, despite huge fans and gun blasts designed to set them whirling about Jane. Vadim resorted to placing bird seed in Jane's costume, but that didn't work either. The stress was so great on Jane that Vadim had to hospitalize her for three days with hypertension and nausea. Finally, lovebirds were found that would cooperate sufficiently to get the scene on film.

94

Vadim was well aware that a large part of the potential audience for *Barbarella* were men who had fantasized over the frequently nude comic-strip heroine, and that they would be anxiously awaiting a glimpse of Jane Fonda *à nu*. Jane was opposed to any prolonged nudity in the film, and Vadim wanted to get the audience's more prurient interests out of the way as early as possible. So he devised a scene to appear beneath the credits, wherein Jane would strip while floating weightless. The scene, Jane was told, would reveal nothing of her private anatomy because of the titles. Vadim's initial print, though, did not hide enough of her to satisfy Jane, and she insisted he redo it. Still, the finished film reveals enough of Jane's attributes to please the most avid skin fancier.

Barbarella was a huge commercial success and a critical failure. Its irreverence and sexiness were perfect for audiences who had had enough of sexual and political hypocrisy, and young people in particular flocked to see it. Older, more established critics looked on it as trash, not good enough to be threatening but not bad enough to be dismissed. Charles Champlin of the Los Angeles *Times* commented, "You could subtitle the film *2002, A Space Idiocy* . . . the whole movie gives weightlessness a new definition . . . It is a special taste, and not for your junior birdmen, but a foolish little something for the big birds."

Jane's performance—which created a real human being in the midst of a cartoon—was praised far more often than the film. Pauline Kael wrote, "Jane Fonda, having sex on the wilted feathers and rough, scroungy furs of *Barbarella* is more charming and fresh and bouncy than ever—the American girl triumphing by her innocence over a lewd comic strip world of the future. She's the only comedienne I know who is sexiest when she is funniest . . . she registers comic disbelief that such naughty things can be happening to her, and then her disbelief changes into an even more comic delight. Her American good-girl innocence makes her a marvelously apt heroine for pornographic comedy. She has the skittish innocence of the teenage voluptuary . . . and that innocent's sense of naughtiness, of being a tarnished lady, keeps her from being just another naked actress."

There were, though, many people who were beginning to think of Jane in just that way, and the situation wasn't helped by a *Newsweek* cover of Jane in the nude, to accompany a story about sex in the movies. Jane's awakening political consciousness would soon be mortified by her participation in films like *Barbarella,* and it wasn't long before she publicly criticized Vadim for his "sexual exploitation of women."

Spirits of the Dead, Jane's next release, is another of her "forgotten" pictures; one recent Fonda biography, otherwise quite thorough, fails to mention it. Its lack of success may have had a lot to do with that, as well as the fact that Jane's story was just one of four in this anthology, based loosely on the tales of Edgar Allen Poe. Vadim directed two segments, one of them Jane's; the others were directed by Louis Malle and Federico Fellini.

Jane played the mysterious horsewoman Frédérique, who has an incestuous relationship with her cousin Wilhelm, who she suspects has been reincarnated as her horse. Here, she practices her archery. With Jane in this photograph is none other than a bearded Andreas Voutsinas.

For their first and only time acting together, Jane and Peter played the incestuous lovers. Jane bristled at the suggestion that casting siblings in such a situation was exploitative: "It was not our intention to 'titillate' this way, and in Europe at least, no one took it like that. Not that I'm against incest, but our style is more direct. When the time comes for incest we will do it head on and leave the titillating for others. Give us credit, at least, for honesty."

OPPOSITE Frédérique tends to her horse/lover; at the end of the tale, she has metamorphosed into a horse herself, in order to rejoin Wilhelm. Peter had wanted to work with Jane for some time, and developed a vehicle for them entitled *The Yin and the Yang,* in which Jane would be cast as Crass Commercialism. Mercifully, perhaps, nothing came of it. But Peter and Jane were becoming closer; he was getting his life together—ironically, with the help of drugs. His first LSD trip, he avowed, had been a revelation to him: "As (it) progressed, I thought about my father and about my relationship with him and my mother and my sister. And suddenly I busted through the whole thing and related to everything. There was no more worry about my father, mother, and sister. I began to really feel on top of all my problems. I had no further relationship with the past, I'd kicked it."

Another time, he said, "I really dig my sister. Probably a great deal more than she digs me, and she *digs* me." But both Jane and Peter were more estranged from their father than ever. "I dig my father, too," Peter added. "I have a great deal of compassion for him, too. I wish he could open his eyes and dig me."

Jane looks fetching in one of the film's many costumes, described by John Simon as "Folies-Bergères medievalism" and by columnist Bob Salmaggi as "way out ultra-ultra *haute monde,* running to thigh-high boots, see-through panelings, chic fur ensembles, all giving extremely generous views of the Fonda anatomy."

With the exception of Fellini's segment, *Spirits of the Dead* was critically panned upon its release in 1968. John Simon, in the New York *Times,* took particular exception to Vadim's direction of Jane's segment: "There may be worse directors than Vadim, but no one can surpass him in spiritual rottenness. His is a megalomaniacal interior decorator's world inhabited by campy marionettes. His orgiasts have sawdust in their heads, veins and glands, and Vadim, for all his sexual shadowboxing, cannot even rise to that nadir of eroticism, dishonest titillation."

Jane, who would soon respond to an interviewer's "How are you this morning?" by replying, "I'm thinking of getting a divorce," would come to agree.

PART FOUR

ACTRESS AND ACTIVIST
1969-76

Fonda addresses an antiwar rally at the University of
South Carolina on May 14, 1970.

If the origins of such things can be traced back to a single event or situation, Jane Fonda's "radicalization" began during an April 1964 trip she took to Russia with Vadim, whose forebears originated there. She was reluctant to go because of the threatening impressions of the Russians she, like most Americans, had been raised on. Her visit was a startling revelation for her. "I couldn't believe it," she said when she returned. "All my life I've been brought up to believe the Russians were some alien, hostile people sitting over there just waiting to swallow up America. Nothing could be further from the truth. I was amazed how friendly and kind and helpful they were. My eyes were really opened to the kind of propaganda we've been exposed to in America."

Over the next four years, Jane was inundated with information that shook her strongly inbred faith in the morality and the veracity of the United States Government. It began with Vadim's associates, leftist French intellectuals with a habitually jaundiced view of America, who continually assaulted Jane's American sensibilities and mocked her naïve defense of her native country.

Jane could dismiss much of what she was hearing as cynical dogma, but it was more difficult to explain away the barrage of news reports emanating from Southeast Asia, where America's military involvement in Vietnam was escalating dramatically. America had become marginally involved in the Vietnamese civil war in the late 1950s, as the French were abandoning the effort as unwinnable. The American position was that if the Communist-supported North Vietnamese were able to take over democratic South Vietnam, other Southeast Asian countries, then countries all over the world, would succumb to Communist takeover, eventually directly threatening American security.

This, the controversial "domino" theory, was difficult for many Americans to accept; Vietnam was thousands of miles away. Without a more direct threat to our security, many people were unable to understand the necessity of this military effort. And when American boys began dying by the thousands in a war that had never been declared and that few could understand the justification for, an increasing number of Americans began to protest against the effort.

The "new generation of Americans" John F. Kennedy had spoken of in his inaugural address were far less willing than their elders to accept what their leaders told them as gospel; many had friends fighting in Vietnam who told them stories of official malfeasance, atrocities, corporate exploitation of the conflict, American lives lost to satisfy a general's ego.

As such stories multiplied, the war began to be seen by many as motivated by nothing so much as macho bravura and capitalist greed.

As the antiwar movement grew, and directly influenced President Lyndon Johnson's decision not to seek a second term, evidence of immorality in the American conduct of the war mushroomed. An "International War Crimes Tribunal" was held in Sweden, led by philosophers Bertrand Russell and Jean-Paul Sartre. The tribunal accused the United States of destroying Vietnam in its attempt to save its people from Communism—people who cared little who governed them, as long as they could live in peace. The tribunal reported that the United States had dropped more than one hundred thousand tons of napalm on the country by 1967, and more explosives than it had dropped on the entire Pacific Theater during World War II. Its report stated, "In the south, the U.S. forces and their docile Saigon allies have herded eight million people, peasants and their families, into barbed wire encampments under the surveillance of the political police. Chemical poisons have been, and are being, used to defoliate and render barren tens of thousands of acres of farmland . . . More than five hundred thousand Vietnamese men, woman and children have perished under this onslaught."

Jane, as were many other Americans, was shocked by the fact that much of the war was being conducted in secret, and that the U.S. Government had lied about and covered up many of its wartime actions. Her confidence in her government was irrevocably shaken by this knowledge; and her opposition to the war was intensified by her pregnancy and the new appreciation of human life that it gave her. "I began to feel a unity with people," she said. "I began to love people, to understand that we do not give life to a human being only to have it killed by B-52 bombs, or to have it jailed by fascists, or to have it destroyed by social injustice . . ."

The birth of her child, her maturation as a woman and the barrage of blows to her most cherished beliefs created tremendous turmoil within Jane. Telling Vadim "I've got to find myself," she accepted an invitation in the fall of 1969 to accompany an acquaintance to India. What she saw there deeply shocked her: "I had never seen people actually dying from starvation or a boy begging with the corpse of a little brother in his arms." When she returned to Beverly Hills the contrast appalled her: "I still had in my eyes the crowds of Bombay, in my nose the smell of Bombay, in my ears the noise of Bombay," she said. "My first day back and I saw those houses in Beverly Hills, those immaculate gardens, those neat, silent streets where the rich drive their big cars and send their children to psychoanalysts and employ exploited Mexican gardeners and black servants."

Jane was experiencing a swirl of new and frightening emotions. And in many ways, so was the country. Most of the antiwar protesters were young people, and their opposition to the war was only one symptom of a deep disenchantment with many of the beliefs their parents cherished. It was as if a Grand Canyon–size generation gap had rent the country. And when young people's heads were broken by police nightsticks outside the Democratic National Convention as thousands protested the nomination of a status-quo presidential candidate, the generation gap turned into a national tragedy.

Richard Nixon, a politician whose career appeared over just a few years earlier, was elected President on a promise to end the war in Vietnam. But rather than seeking peace, he escalated the bombing in Vietnam and secretly extended it to Cambodia. He arrogantly inflamed the national unrest by announcing that he would be too busy watching football to pay attention to a huge antiwar rally in Washington, and he called protesters against the war "bums." It was all too much for Jane. The more she heard about the horrors of the war, exploitation of American Indians, atrocities committed against black Americans, exploitation of Mexicans, women, and workers—the angrier she became. As her anger grew, it was in part directed against herself: what had her life accomplished? Was she just a rich dilettante, a sexy pinup in the movies? Jane told herself that the answer was no. And she would do something to prove it—to herself and to the world.

Fonda as the defeated, suicidal Gloria in *They Shoot Horses, Don't They?* (1969), the film that would establish her as one of America's foremost actresses. Horace McCoy's 1935 novel told the bitter story of a group of downtrodden Depression-era misfits who enter a grueling dance marathon in order to win desperately needed money. Gloria, just released from a hospital where she recovered from a suicide attempt after being jilted, has come to Hollywood to pursue the stardom she has dreamed about while reading movie magazines. The marathon is crushing for Gloria, both physically and spiritually; she sees corruption among its promoters and utter hopelessness among its participants. She convinces a young man who has befriended her that he must assist her in committing suicide and help her out of her misery: "They shoot horses, don't they?"

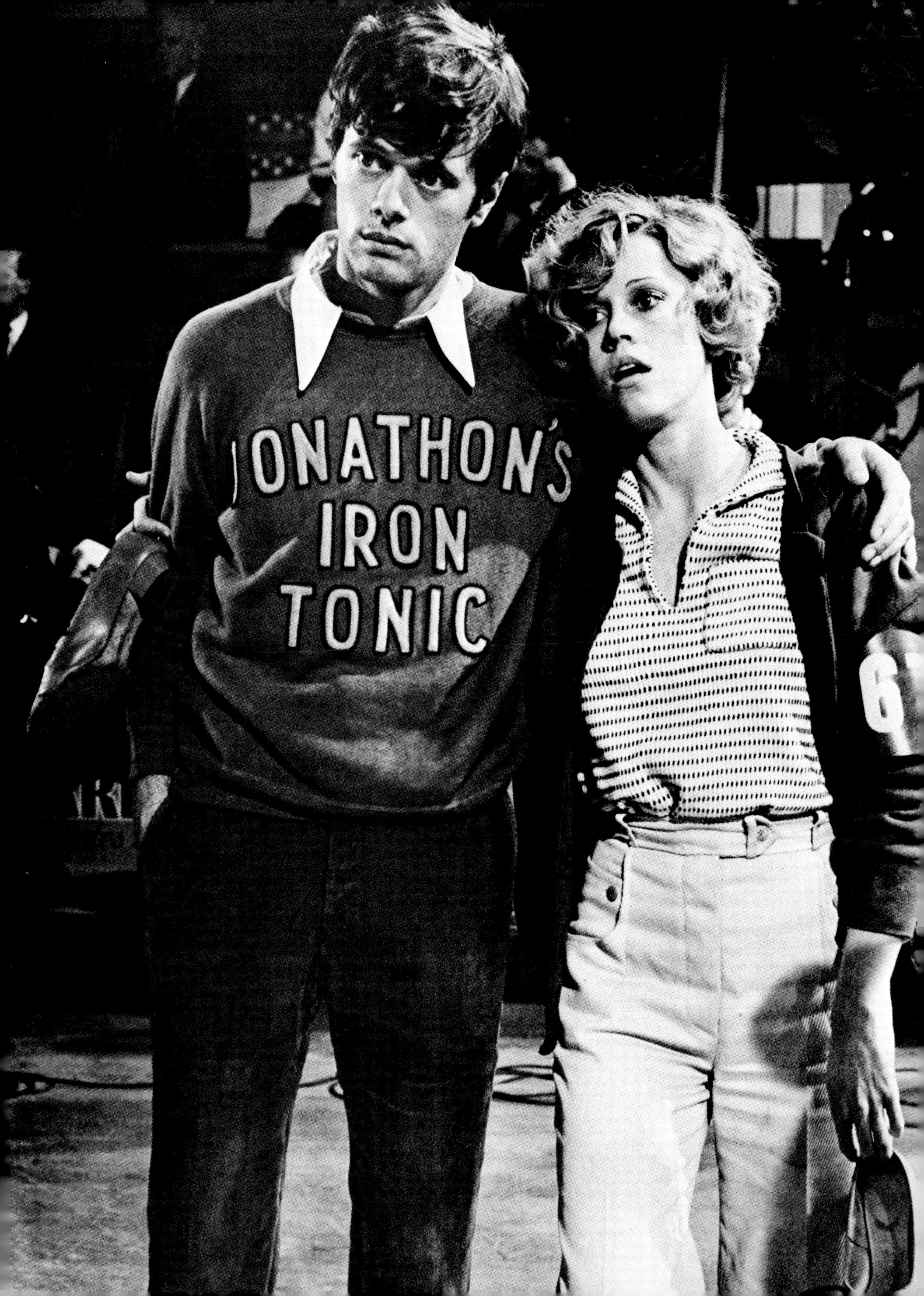
JONATHON'S
IRON
TONIC

OPPOSITE With Michael Sarrazin as Robert, her marathon partner and the man who helps Gloria end her grim existence. McCoy's novel, not a success when it was published in America (at the height of the Depression and the marathon craze) became a cult classic in Europe during the sixties, where it was hailed by Albert Camus as "the first existential novel to come out of America" and was seen as an indictment of America's capitalist system. McCoy's marathon was a metaphor for the Depression and an indictment of the deep-rooted societal ills that caused it. Jane's new social consciousness was intrigued by the parallels between McCoy's world and her own: "The war we're going through now," she said, "our country has never gone through such a long, agonizing experience, except for the Depression. The Depression is the closest America ever came before to a

national disaster . . . Perhaps audiences—especially kids—will be able to come away from seeing *They Shoot Horses* with the feeling that if we could pull out of the Depression, we can pull out of the mess we're in now."

ABOVE Jane enjoys a rare light moment between takes. Although her role was adversely affecting her marriage, Jane knew that she was giving the performance of her life—and so did Sydney Pollack, who had nothing but admiration for his star. "This was her chance really to make an indelible mark as a character that was fully done, fully executed, and she held nothing back. There was no vanity in the performance, no self-preservation. There was no hiding in it. She went all the way."

Jane knew that the role of Gloria was a once-in-a-lifetime opportunity for her to prove herself as a dramatic actress. "I was sick and tired of being thought of as a sex symbol," she said. If only for this reason, she would have approached the role with extreme seriousness. But Jane Fonda was at a point in her life where she identified very closely with Gloria. She was unsure of her position in the world, she was deeply troubled by the grim plight of the people she had seen in India, she feared for the fate of her country in its involvement in a war she was beginning to see as immoral. Gloria's dark and disturbed spirit began seeping into Jane's; it was more than just the fact that director Sydney Pollack, to add realism to his film, had decided to shoot in continuity, and to have his actors actually suffer the strain of marathon dancing. Her coworkers noticed it immediately. One of them said, "During the week it was hard to tell the difference between Jane and Gloria. Off the set she walked like her, talked like her, mumbled like her. She had this perpetual tired, vacuous expression on her face . . . she got thinner and thinner—you could almost see the weight melting away . . ."

Jane was disturbed by the hold Gloria had taken of her, but there was nothing she could do to shake it. Upset that she was bringing Gloria's grimness home with her, she moved herself into her dressing trailer full time, succumbing completely to the role. "Gloria was such a desperate, negative, depressed person. Gradually, I let myself become that way, too. How could I go home like that? I'd walk in the door and *aarrgh!* So I stayed away."

The changes Jane had been going through as a woman and as a person had already weakened her relationship with Vadim, and her immersion in *They Shoot Horses* further eroded the marriage. Vadim wrote in his autobiography, ". . . she was living her part with almost morbid intensity. A tenuous shadow, an indefinable sense of drifting apart, as though some cold barrier was growing between us, made me feel that I was living a waking nightmare . . . The erosion of love is a sordid, shabby, absurd thing. A shameful and useless sickness. It is not even a lost battle, it is a cancer that eats away body, soul and mind. No one ever completely recovers from it."

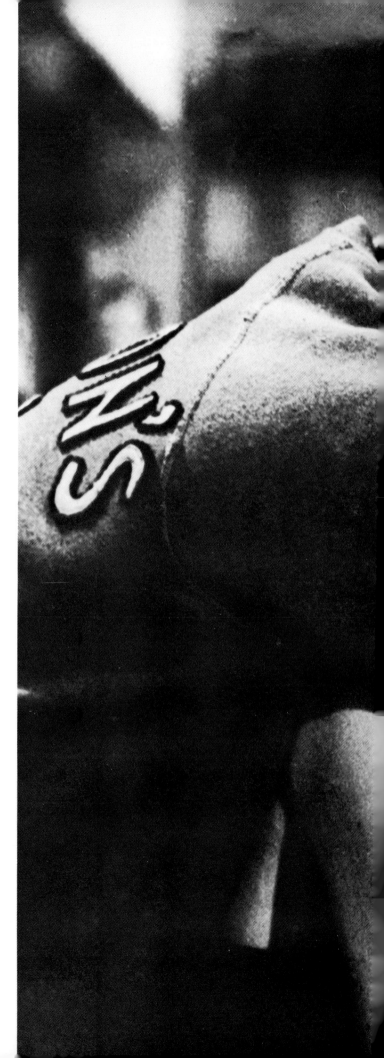

Jane's performance in *They Shoot Horses, Don't They?* stunned many audiences and critics. Nothing she had done before prepared one for the intensity, the depth, the authenticity of her portrayal of Gloria. Although the movie was frequently criticized, most often for its deadening nihilism, Jane's work was universally praised. "As Gloria," John Simon wrote, "that fine little actress, Jane Fonda, graduates into a fine big actress . . . [She] here gives an antipodal performance: there is none of the glitter, kittenishness or jollity that have been her specialties in the past . . . and there is something about her very toughness that repeatedly moves us . . ."

Jane received her first major acting award for *They Shoot Horses,* the New York Film Critics' designation as Best Actress, and her first Academy Award nomination. The consensus was that Fonda was a shoo-in for the Oscar, but the award that April went to Maggie Smith in *The Prime of Miss Jean Brodie.* Many observers felt that Jane had been denied the award because of her increasingly public expression of her radical views and a run-in a few weeks earlier with military police. If there was one thing Academy members didn't want to do, the reasoning went, it was to afford Jane Fonda a world-wide forum in which to spout antiwar rhetoric.

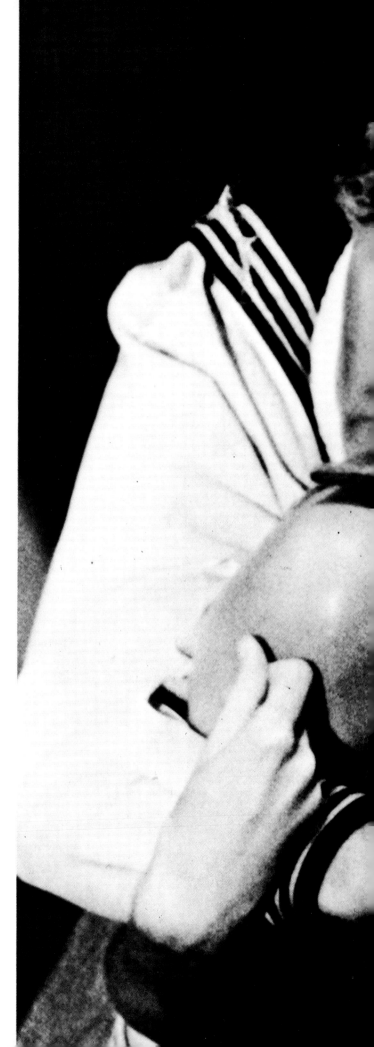

March 16, 1970: Jane leads a group of Indian demonstrators in a march on the United States Courthouse in Seattle, Washington, to protest their expulsion from Fort Lawton a week earlier. Jane's support of the Indian rights cause had begun at the deserted Alcatraz Prison in San Francisco Bay in January, which had been "occupied" by Indians since November 1969 in protest of their treatment by the U.S. Government. Hearing of the takeover, and learning about the oppression of Indians in America, Jane took up her very first "radical" cause: "I learned about the genocide that had taken place, that is still taking place, the infamies we had done to the Indians in the name of efficiency, in the interest of white farmers. And I learned that the senators who are supposed to defend the Indians haven't done a thing."

After talking to the militants holding Alcatraz, Jane traveled to Fort Lawton, where Indians were laying claim to the land on which the Army Reserve base was situated. Jane and dozens of others were arrested by military police and expelled from the fort. At this demonstration the following week, picketers protested the Army's action, and Jane announced that she and attorney Mark Lane had filed suit against the Army, claiming they had been illegally barred from the fort and demanding access to it and other bases.

FOLLOWING PAGE Jane raises a clenched fist as one hundred thousand people scream "Power to the People!" at an antiwar demonstration in Washington, D.C., on May 9, 1970. She began her address to the crowd with, "Welcome, fellow bums!" a reference to President Nixon's characterization of antiwar demonstrators. She fired up the crowd with an impassioned speech against America's "immoral" war, but urged them to avoid violence.

By now, Jane's antiwar activities and social protests were getting tremendous media exposure: she was a glamorous Hollywood star taking controversial public stands. As such, she was a lightning rod for both supporters and detractors of her cause: those who agreed with her saw her as a symbol of the public's increasing acceptance of their stands; those who disagreed with her saw her as an example of the ignorance and dilettantism of the antiwar movement. As would soon become clear, Jane Fonda's activism fired up a disproportionate emotionalism in all segments of society—even the highest levels of government.

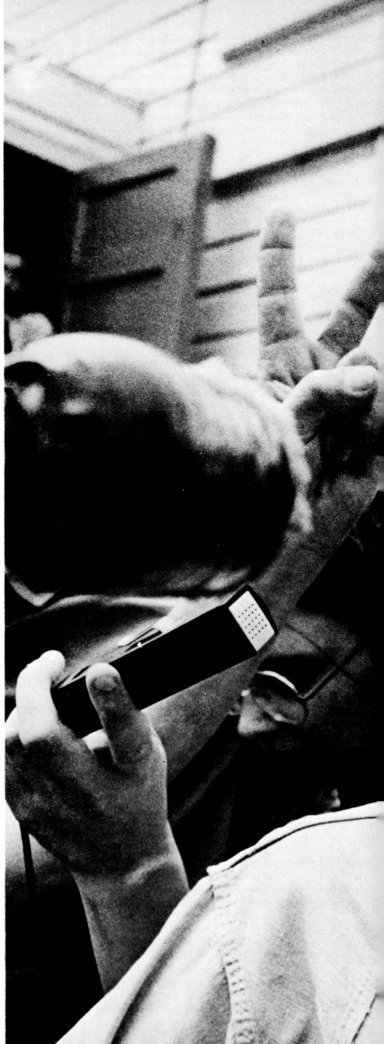

As part of a cross-country automobile tour of college campuses and army bases with a friend, French leftist Elisabeth Vailland, Jane distributed antiwar leaflets at Fort Hood, Texas. After refusing to cease handing out the leaflets, Jane was placed under arrest by military police, who took mug photos and fingerprinted her. Here, she talks to reporters after her release. Commenting bitterly on her arrest by the military, Jane said, "Bob Hope was greeted differently by the local branch of the military-industrial complex. But then, I did not come here to glamorize war or to urge young men to fight . . . I'm campaigning on behalf of human rights, whether they be Indians, GIs or whatever." She charged that GIs were being put on planes to Vietnam at gunpoint if they were caught dissenting, and that the authorities were fearful that her agitation among enlisted men threatened the military establishment: "If they're getting uptight about my being on an Army base, it means they're worried about something, as well they should be."

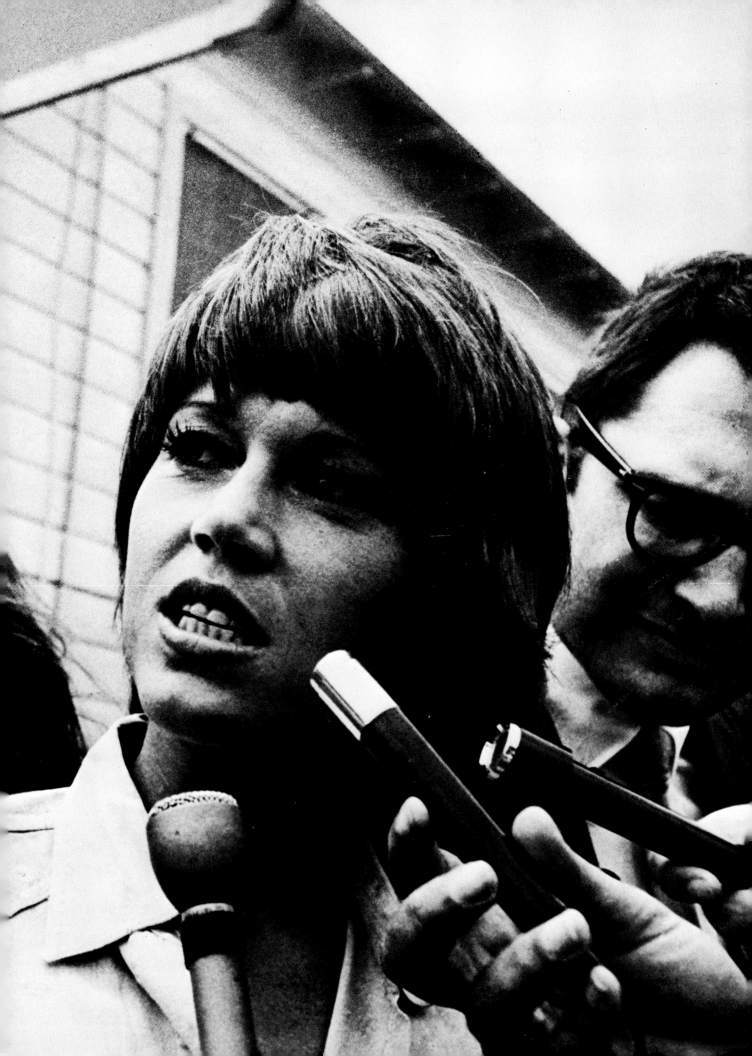

During the summer of 1970, Jane took a break from her radical activities for a Saint-Tropez vacation with Vadim and Vanessa. Although both Roger and Jane considered their marriage over after *They Shoot Horses* filming ended, they stayed together for some time for the sake of their child and, although separated for most of 1971 and all of 1972, they were not officially divorced until January 1973.

OPPOSITE Handcuffed, Jane is led to jail in Cleveland on November 3, 1970, after her arrest at Hopkins Airport on charges of drug smuggling and assaulting a police officer. Returning from Canada after a college speaking engagement, Jane was stopped upon disembarking from her plane, for no apparent reason. Her baggage was searched, and numerous vials of pills—which the customs officer took to be illegal contraband—were seized. Jane protested that they were vitamins, but she was detained and denied a

chance to use the bathroom until police matrons could search her. Infuriated, she pushed past several officers, a scuffle broke out, and Jane was arrested.

The government's smuggling case against Jane evaporated when the lab report established that the "contraband" was vitamins and prescribed Valium, and her lawyer's insistence that she was on a secret list of Nixon enemies targeted for harassment threatened to embarrass the Administration (the Watergate hearings three years later would prove the existence of the list). The government moved to have its charges against Jane dismissed. The assault charges, brought by the state of Ohio, were also dismissed when it was discovered that the "assaulted" officer lacked the power to arrest Jane within the U.S. Customs Hall.

This firsthand experience with political persecution, not surprisingly, had the effect of further radicalizing Jane and strengthening her opposition to the Nixon administration.

118

OPPOSITE Fonda as Bree Daniel, the hip, cynical New York call girl in Alan Pakula's film *Klute*. Pakula has said, "It's a film I would not have done without Jane," and it is easy to see why. Her inspired, stunningly realistic characterization of Bree as an intelligent, nervous, ambitious, sad, manipulative, frightened, and vulnerable young woman elevated the picture from an average crime thriller to a classic study of a certain kind of woman in our society, and the psychological terrors—from both within and without—that torment her.

ABOVE With Donald Sutherland as John Klute, a private investigator looking for a missing friend who

had been a customer of Bree's. At first contemptuous of the straitlaced Klute, Bree comes to depend on him as her sense of control over her life is shattered by the terrorizing phone calls of a sadistic killer. Eventually, the two fall in love, a situation that further disturbs Bree, since she has never let a man "get to" her before.

Fonda and Sutherland had been friends and neighbors in Malibu, and they shared radical views. Separated from Vadim, Jane was open to a new relationship, and she and Sutherland began a romance.

FOLLOWING PAGES Bree wears the glamorous gown one of her customers requires.

121

On a Greenwich Village rooftop, Jane helps Pakula set up a shot. Jane saw the character of Bree Daniel as an example of the sexist exploitation of women in contemporary society, and this political aspect of the film helped her decide to do it. Her research included spending time with prostitutes, so that she could better understand them and their world. It was still another eye-opening experience for her; she began to understand the developing women's movement: "My whole thinking changed. I began to realize that this particular revolution is not only their revolution, it's my revolution, too. I mean, if I don't fight it, nobody else is going to . . . I was able to understand, for the first time, my mother; I was able to understand my sister, myself, my friends, the women I know."

OPPOSITE Pakula was relieved to find Jane so immersed in her character, because by the time filming began she was involved in a great many diverse political causes. "I was concerned that her mind was not going to be on the film," he said. "But she has this extraordinary kind of concentration. She can . . . make endless phone calls . . . and seem to be totally uninterested in the film. But when you say, 'We're ready for you, Jane,' she says, 'All right, give me a few minutes.' She just stands quietly for three minutes and concentrates, and then she's totally and completely in the film, and nothing else exists . . . It's a gift good actors have; she has it to an extraordinary degree."

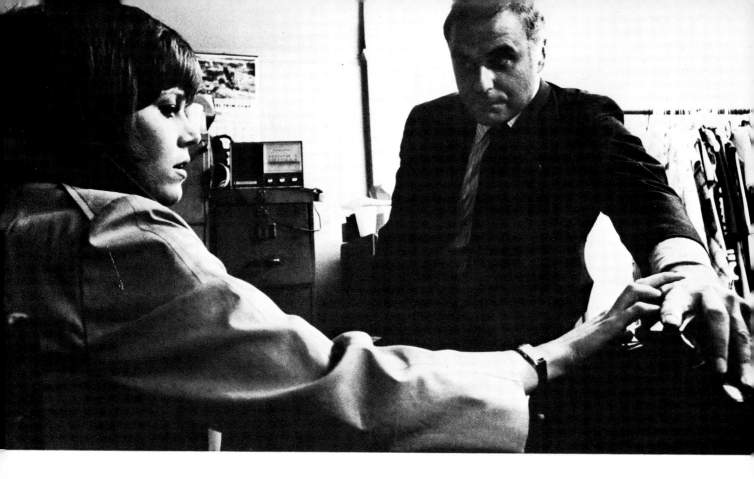

The shattering climax of *Klute:* Bree is trapped by her tormenter and is forced to listen to a tape-recording of his sadistic murder of her friend. Jane's enactment of this scene, in which she sobs until mucus drips from her nose, stunned audiences with its grimness. Jane, in fact, had never heard the tape before she performed the scene, which Pakula shot in one take and did not edit. When *Klute* was released, it was abundantly clear that Jane Fonda had become one of this country's best actresses, and that *They Shoot Horses* wasn't just a fluke. Pauline Kael offered a particularly cogent analysis of Fonda's achievement: "She disappears into Bree, the call-girl, so totally that her performance is very pure—unadorned by 'acting' . . . she never stands outside Bree, she gives herself over to the role, and yet she isn't *lost* in it —she's fully in control, and her means are extraordinarily economical. She has somehow got a plane of acting at which even the closest close-up never reveals a false thought . . ."

OPPOSITE April 10, 1972: Jane holds her Academy Award as the Best Actress of 1971 for *Klute.* Although Jane was now more controversial by far than she had been two years earlier when many felt her political views cost her an Oscar, there was no denying her

this time. Still, there was once again fear that she would use her acceptance speech to launch a shrill denunciation of the war, and she in fact had been pressured by her radical associates to make a political statement should she win. Her father implored her not to, and despite their increased estrangement over Jane's political stands (he had referred to her in an interview as "my alleged daughter"), she was won over by his argument that her views, already well known, would be more eloquently conveyed if left unspoken that night.

Jane also considered refusing the award as a protest, but, "a woman who is much wiser than I am said to me, 'It's really typical of the bourgeois middle-class family girl to want to refuse the Oscar.' " Jane was also convinced that accepting the award would remove some of the stigma that conservatives had attached to her as a wild-eyed radical.

When her name was called, Jane accepted her award, and, as millions waited to see what she would do next, she spoke calmly: "There's a great deal to say, and I'm not going to say it tonight." Her graciousness made a good impression on many Americans, who came to see her as much softer than she had been portrayed in the more conservative media. The good will her Oscar-win generated for her proved to be short-lived, however: less than three months later, she would travel to Hanoi.

In mid-July 1972, Jane flew to the capital city of North Vietnam for a firsthand look at what the war was doing to that country. She toured bombed-out ruins, hospitals, and refugee camps; she met with American prisoners of war willing to see her, who told her that they were treated well by the North Vietnamese and that their most fervent wish was that President Nixon be defeated for reelection in November so that the war might end.

Jane was horrified by the destruction of lives, property, and landscape that had been wrought by Ameri-

can bombs; she was particularly dismayed by the American bombing of North Vietnam's dike system. She felt that America was intent on destroying an entire country in an undeclared war for which there was no valid justification.

OPPOSITE RIGHT Jane visits the bomb-damaged Truong Dinh residential center in the Nai Ba Trung District in Hanoi on July 17.

Feeling that she might be able to appeal directly to the American men dropping the bombs, Jane made a series of ten broadcasts over Radio Hanoi, urging American soldiers to renounce the war. On one, she said, "Tonight when you are alone, ask yourselves: What are you? Accept no ready answers fed to you by rote from basic training . . . I know that if you saw and if you knew the Vietnamese under peaceful conditions, you would hate the men who are sending you on bombing missions . . . Have you any idea what your bombs are doing when you pull the levers and push the buttons?" On another broadcast, she accused President Nixon of "betraying everything the American people have at heart, betraying the long tradition of freedom and democracy."

Jane's visit to Hanoi—and especially her broadcasts—outraged supporters of the war, who labeled her "Hanoi Jane" and demanded that she be indicted for treason. The rage that Jane's action elicited in many people cannot be overstated; they saw her as a "pinko slut" who appeared nude in movies, smoked pot, smuggled drugs, used profanity publicly and now, worst of all, was aiding and abetting the enemy during wartime. Several members of the United States Congress called for her prosecution as a traitor.

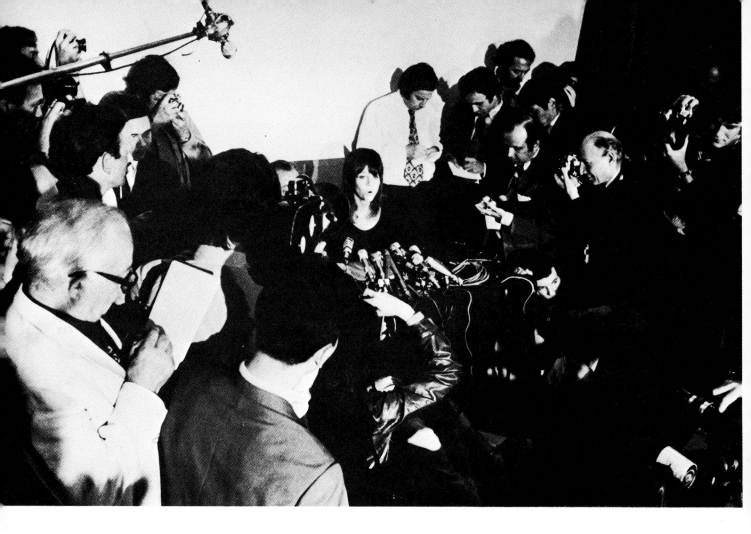

At a tumultuous, hastily called press conference in Paris immediately upon her return from North Vietnam, Jane defended herself against all charges. "What is a traitor?" she asked angrily. "I cried every day I was in Vietnam. I cried for America. The bombs are falling on.Vietnam, but it is an American tragedy . . . The bombing is all the more awful when you can see the little faces, see the women say, 'Thank you, American people, for speaking out against the war.' I believe the people in this country who are speaking out are the real patriots."

The reporters, though, were hostile. Wasn't she seeing only one side of the issue? "There *are* no both sides in this question," she responded, stressing her belief that America was entirely at fault for the war. When one reporter suggested that she was being used by the North Vietnamese for propaganda purposes, she shot back, "Do you think the North Vietnamese blow up their own hospitals? Are they bombing their own dikes? Are they mutilating their own women and children to impress me? Anyone who speaks out against this war is carrying on propaganda —propaganda for peace, propaganda against death, propaganda for life!"

OPPOSITE At the Paris press conference, Fonda screens a film she made in Hanoi depicting American prisoners of war speaking out against the United States war effort. She denied that the North Vietnamese mistreated Americans held as prisoners; she asserted rather that North Vietnamese prisoners held in American camps were routinely tortured, and that some were thrown from airplanes as lessons to the others. Jane's insistence that it was only Americans, and never North Vietnamese, who practiced torture of prisoners further inflamed conservative opinion against her. Her father, although displeased by much of what Jane was saying and doing, refused to be caught up in her public condemnation; he said that he resented people who expected him to denounce her and added that in fact he was proud of her for having the courage of her convictions.

Fonda and Sutherland attend a screening of their new film, *FTA,* in Westwood, California, on July 31, less than a week after Jane's Paris press conference.

ABOVE RIGHT As Jane left the theater following the screening, a group of angry demonstrators confronted her. One held a nude poster of Jane popular in the late sixties—over which he had pasted the legend NAKED CAME THE TRAITOR—and pressed it against the windshield of the departing car.

Despite the visceral hatred that Jane's trip to Hanoi stirred up against her, congressional attempts to prosecute her for treason failed for the same reason that the Vietnam conflict was so unpopular: the war had never been formally declared, and was therefore technically illegal.

OPPOSITE LEFT A skit from the American International Pictures release *FTA.* Since mid-1970, Jane had been touring GI coffeehouses—off-base retreats where service men could get a respite from Army restrictions—with a satirical antimilitary show, meant to be something of an answer to Bob Hope's famous tours. The troupe's name, FTA, got a laugh from the outset, since every GI knew it as the traditional acronym for Fuck The Army. The troupe, of course, insisted it stood for Free Theater Associates, but when pressed said it was an acronym for Free The Army—which is what they hoped to do by presenting these shows.

The program consisted of songs, skits, and raps with the audience. Among those who participated at one point or another during the eighteen months the troupe toured were Peter Boyle, Holly Near, Dick Gregory, "Country Joe" McDonald, and writers Barbara Garson *(MacBird),* Jules Feiffer, and Herb Gardner.

ABOVE RIGHT Michael Alaimo joins Jane for another roast of the military establishment. The FTA shows were very popular among dissident GIs, whose numbers were growing—but many in the audiences were there to report back to army officials, who forwarded accounts of Jane's statements to the Secret Service.

The relatively minor distribution company AIP was the only one willing to take on *FTA*, and it lasted only a few days in most markets—in Los Angeles, in fact, the film was pulled overnight from its theater. It was reviewed only sparsely, and is another largely forgotten Fonda film (it is not likely to show up on television). Roger Greenspan gave *FTA* one of its few in-depth reviews, in the New York *Times:* "The film divides its attention pretty evenly between the performers and their audience, and a lot of time is given to interviews with dissident or disillusioned servicemen . . . So much time is given to the audience, whose insights, though real, are neither original nor profound, that the actual performance comes across in scattered bits and pieces . . . there are a few good things . . . some hints at lively routines, an occasional glimpse of deep happiness in the eyes of Holly Near and Miss Fonda. But the spirit of FTA must lie elsewhere, in other times and special places. For all its agility and pressing close-ups, the film doesn't capture the spirit."

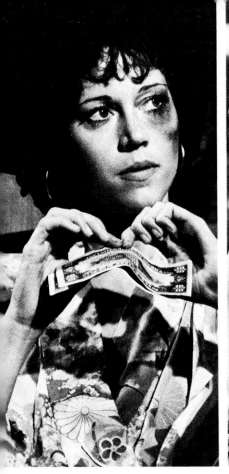

Jane as Iris, a part-time prostitute, in *Steelyard Blues*. Despite her Oscar win, Jane was finding it increasingly difficult to get work in Hollywood because she had become so controversial; nothing scares off Hollywood executives more than controversy. Although there was never an official "blacklisting" of Jane to compare with those spawned by Senator Joseph McCarthy's witch-hunt of Communists in the early 1950s, there can be no question that she was denied work because of her political views. Her professional limbo later became known as her "graylisting."

Had more scripts been coming her way, it is unlikely Jane would have agreed to star in the film, a first-time directing effort by Alan Myerson, one of the FTA troupe. It was something of a family affair, with other members of FTA participating, in front of and behind the cameras.

ABOVE RIGHT With costar Donald Sutherland. *Steelyard Blues* was an amateurish comedy about a group of misfits—each one an affront to the Establishment—who try to fix up an old plane in order to get away from it all. Jane must have cringed at the Warner Bros. publicity release describing the film: "A wacky, anti-establishment comedy about a band of misfits who outwit the law in the merry and sympathetic tradition of *Bonnie and Clyde.*"

OPPOSITE *Steelyard Blues,* which followed closely on the heels of *FTA,* suffered a similarly ignominious fate at the box office, and its lack of quality was particularly disappointing after *They Shoot Horses* and *Klute. Motion Picture* magazine's review noted, "Jane Fonda, who has played happily amoral kooks in the past, now seems obsessed with hookers as some kind of symbol of oppressed womanhood, and the role is getting tiresome. After her significant portrayal in *Klute,* why repeat herself in a film that isn't even worth the watching? *Steelyard Blues* is almost as big a bomb as her recent *FTA,* if that is possible."

Pauline Kael added: "Jane Fonda (is) just doing a long walk-through. She has charm—even without a character to play—but her and Sutherland's roguish complacency at being hip outlaws in a straight society isn't the charming nonsense they mean it to be. Their little digs and grimaces about the meanness of the straights are almost a parody of their offscreen characters, and it's embarrassing to watch them, because they've turned blithe exuberance into cant."

Stockholm, Sweden, December 1972: Jane wipes her face after a young woman emptied a can of red paint over her as she marched in an antiwar demonstration. Fonda reacted with aplomb and shortly thereafter addressed a throng of six thousand peace protesters, charging that Richard Nixon's "concept of peace is to escalate the killing. The U.S. election did not give Nixon a mandate to carry on the war."

OPPOSITE TOP Immigration officials at London's Heathrow Airport search the luggage of Jane and her boyfriend, Tom Hayden, as they leave Britain to return to America on December 28, 1972. After leaving Sweden, the couple had encountered difficulty in entering the United Kingdom for an antiwar conference; immigration officials quizzed them at length, and they were granted only a short visit.

Jane had met Hayden early in 1971 at a peace rally at the University of Michigan. He was impressed by the fact that she was more than a living sex doll ("I thought she was as high strung as any wire and extremely nervous, almost out of her body. I'd never encountered anyone like that before"); she had read several of his books and was fascinated by his credentials as a revolutionary. He had founded the preeminent radical group of the 1960s, Students for a Democratic Society, and became one of the principal defendants at the trial of the Chicago Seven, men accused of disrupting the 1968 Democratic Convention in that city. Although he had been convicted and sentenced, his appeal was successful because the trial was deemed a mockery of justice, and it was clear to impartial observers that what had begun as a peaceful demonstration was turned into a bloody riot by the police, not the protesters.

OPPOSITE BOTTOM Fonda looks affectionately at Hayden during one of the stops on their ninety-city tour of the country—sponsored by their new organization, the Indochina Peace Campaign—during which they showed slides of Jane's trip to Hanoi, spoke against the war and answered questions. After their 1971 meeting, the couple did not see each other again until the spring of 1972, when they began their relationship. Hayden was an intelligent, witty man, whose ability to guide Jane through her radical course was as strong as Voutsinas's and Vadim's ability to draw out her acting talent. No matter how much she had developed as her own woman, it was said, Jane still needed a strong man in her life, and Hayden—a hero to the people who were most important to her now—was her perfect complement. After their second meeting, Jane says, "I came home to my roommate and I said, 'I'm going to marry him.' I just *knew* it. He was stronger than I was, he was one of the only men that I'd ever met that I knew I would never be bored with—and I knew he wouldn't be intimidated by me." And on top of everything else, she adds, "I thought he was funny. Not too many people were funny in those days, but Tom had a sense of humor, he laughed a lot—which I found thoroughly engaging." On January 21, 1973, Hayden married Jane—who was four months pregnant—in her Laurel Canyon home. The ceremony was attended by her father and his fifth wife, Shirlee; Peter and his second wife, Rebecca; and more than one hundred other people.

Six days later, a ceasefire agreement was signed in Vietnam, ending twenty years of American involvement and making that war the first in American history to be "lost."

Jane returned to the world of the French cinema for her next film, *Tout Va Bien (Everything's Okay)*, directed by the esteemed Jean-Luc Godard *(Breathless)*. Godard was a Marxist who shared many of Jane's beliefs; the story, in fact, was reportedly inspired by Jane's radicalization: a filmmaker (Yves Montand) and his journalist wife (Jane) visit a sausage factory to do some filming. While they are there, the workers (all women) take over the factory to protest working conditions. By the next morning, Jane's character has been radicalized to the point of seeing her management-sympathetic husband as a symbol of the repressive bourgeiosie, and their marriage is threatened.

Jane was thrilled at first to be working with Godard, whom she called "the only person I've ever met who's truly revolutionary." But she was quickly disillusioned by the way Godard treated her. "Godard really hates people," she said. "Especially women. He never told me what was going on in *Tout Va Bien,* and when I realized, I wanted to leave, but he threatened to rough me up if I did. It was a terrible experience . . . A true revolutionary has to care about *people . . .*"

Tout Va Bien became Jane's third critical and financial disaster within a year. It received scant distribution in the United States, and most reviews were scathing in their condemnation of Godard's heavy-handed attempts to proselytize. *"Tout Va Bien,"* wrote *Samedi et Dimanche* magazine, "is a tedious, pretentious, boring and unconvincing political self-indulgence for those before and behind the camera . . . No one in their right mind would pay money to be preached at so shamelessly."

Jane's troubles with Godard did not end with filming. About the time *Tout Va Bien* was released, Godard exhibited a short film called *Letter to Jane.* It consisted of nothing but a photograph of Jane in Hanoi, listening to residents describe the horrors of the American bombing, and a soundtrack scolding her for speaking for the North Vietnamese: ". . . one must say as an American, 'I'll keep my mouth shut because I admit I have got nothing to say about this . . . I have to listen . . . because I am not a part of Southeast Asia.' "

It was criticism from a surprising source, but it does not appear to have chastened Jane in the least.

A disgusted Jane turns away from conservative California politician Robert Dornan in the Los Angeles City Council Chambers, May 3, 1973. Jane had appeared as the Council members considered a recommendation to censure her for her charge that returning American prisoners of war were lying about torture at the hands of the North Vietnamese. She presented an Indochina Peace Campaign report questioning the POW statements. Dornan blasted her for "telling lies," and the City Council sent the motion to committee for further consideration. On June 28, they announced that such a censure was "beyond the scope of city business," and the matter was dropped.

Jane's insistence that the North Vietnamese had done nothing wrong during all the years of the war, and her charges that POW reports to the contrary were orchestrated lies to make the military and the Administration look good, were met with a new wave of outrage against her: one U.S. congressman "nominated" her for an award for "the rottenest, most miserable performance by any one individual American in the history of our country," and the Indiana State Senate adopted a resolution censuring her for her statements.

But Jane was convinced of the fundamental goodness of the Vietnamese people, and because the war had indeed been proven to be immoral, illegal, tragically wasteful and unwinnable, Jane felt vindicated. Her resolve against all official versions of what happened hardened—and even in the face of uncontrovertible evidence of North Vietnamese violation of human rights against their own Boat People, who were cast adrift and left to die, Jane has never re-canted her loyalty to North Vietnam. She did, however, contribute money to help the Boat People and at one point said she had no intention of becoming an "apologist" for North Vietnam.

OPPOSITE October 18, 1973: Jane displays a secret Department of Justice dossier on her personal activities, supplied to her by columnist Jack Anderson. Jane learned that her worst suspicions had been true: she had been followed and spied upon, her phones had been tapped, her mail intercepted. Informants were paid to supply the FBI with detailed accounts of her activities and statements. The Nixon administration attempted to have the Internal Revenue Service audit her tax returns, but the IRS refused.

Worst of all, in June 1970, FBI director J. Edgar Hoover directed his subversive activities chief in Los Angeles to dispatch a letter to a *Daily Variety* columnist describing a fundraiser for the radical Black Panther Party, at which Jane and one of the Panthers led the group in chanting "We will kill Richard Nixon."

Although Jane was a Panther supporter, this meeting had never taken place, and Hoover's memorandum was a blatant attempt to "frame" Jane Fonda. Supported by the American Civil Liberties Union, Jane filed a $1 million lawsuit against the Nixon administration, charging that her First, Fourth, Fifth, and Ninth amendment rights had been violated. The suit was not settled until six years later and, although Jane received no money, she considered it a "moral victory" because it included a pledge by the FBI that all such activities—whether directed at Jane or anyone else—would cease.

On location in Norway to film Ibsen's *A Doll's House.*
The nineteenth-century drama about a young
woman trapped by the sexist mores of her era was a
perfect vehicle for Jane, and Joseph Losey seemed
the perfect director—he had been a victim of the
McCarthy blacklisting, and had re-established himself in England. But this would prove the most difficult and strife-ridden film Jane had ever made. She
had definite ideas about the script, which she felt
should be as strongly feminist as possible, and she
feared that Losey was turning it away from the heroine, Nora, and toward her husband. Losey considered her meddlesome. "I have directed the most
temperamental stars of all time," he said, "but I have
never encountered the likes of Jane Fonda. She was
spending most of her time working on her political
speeches instead of learning her lines, and making
innumerable phone calls about her political activities."

Jane retorted, in an interview with Molly Haskell
for *The Village Voice,* "We tried to get at least the most
important things back in [the script] . . . they inter-
preted anything we did as simply wanting more lines
to say. They painted it as a conspiracy of dykes gang-
ing up on 'us poor men.' Every day there would be
some inscription on the camera about Women's Lib
. . . I was completely professional. I never came late
and I always knew my lines . . . (a) well-disciplined
actress who had some ideas about the play, that he
couldn't handle. And this from a man who calls himself a progressive, a Marxist."

OPPOSITE With David Warner as her husband. Because of Jane's "graylisting" (which had gotten considerably darker after her visit to Hanoi; one studio
head was reported to have said, "The bitch will never
be allowed inside my gates again"), theatrical distribution for *A Doll's House* was impossible to obtain. It
was finally picked up as a movie special by ABC television and aired on December 23, 1973. Although
both the film and Jane were praised by the critics,
ratings were low.

When she completed filming *A Doll's House,* Jane
found that scripts were simply not being submitted
to her, and she did not star in another film for four
years. She withdrew from public view, making a
home in Santa Monica, California, with Tom Hayden, giving birth to her son, Troy, on July 7, 1973,
and turning most of her attention from the Indochina Peace Campaign to the formation of a new
organization—the Campaign for Economic Democracy, designed to redirect the energies of the left to
the plight of the disadvantaged. This crusade would
become Jane's most enduring passion.

March 14, 1974: Jane and Tom display a telegram they received from Cambodian Prince Norodom Sihanouk in response to their inquiries on how to end the fighting in Cambodia. Jane charged that with the end of the Vietnam war, America had become similarly involved in the Cambodian civil war: "Since the official end of the war in Vietnam, over 80,000 civilians have been killed, over one million refugees created and over 300 people are still being killed daily in Cambodia. The planes, the bombs and the bullets are ours . . . if the American people just knew, they wouldn't stand for their tax dollars being spent like that. And that's why the government has to lie about what they're doing."

Sihanouk suggested that American planes be used to transport his foe Lon Nol out of the country. Within a few years, all American involvement in Indochina had ended.

OPPOSITE Tom tends to Troy while Jane speaks to guests at a December 1975 fundraiser at their home for Tom's upcoming campaign for the 1976 California Democratic senatorial nomination. By challenging moderate incumbent Senator John Tunney for the nomination, Hayden was embarking on a highly quixotic campaign, particularly in light of his and Jane's controversial reputations. Although the facts revealed about America's conduct of the Vietnam War had vindicated many of Jane's positions, there was still a large body of public resentment against her—and Tom.

Still, Hayden's effort garnered him a highly respectable 40 percent of the vote—and paved the way for the political rehabilitation of both him and his wife.

146

OPPOSITE Jane plays the relatively small part of Night in George Cukor's film *The Blue Bird,* based on the fairy-tale play of Maurice Maeterlinck, in which two young children set out to find the Blue Bird of Happiness and meet a series of strange and wonderful personages along the way. Cast along with Jane in the film were Elizabeth Taylor, Ava Gardner, Cicely Tyson, Robert Morley, and Will Geer. The movie was an unprecedented cooperation between America and the Soviet Union, filmed in Russia and using Soviet technicians and sets. Jane spent six weeks in Russia; at first she was accompanied by Tom and a friend, Troy, and Tom's mother, but Tom was reportedly so upset by the bourgeois attitudes of the average Russian that he and his friend left within a few days.

The Blue Bird appears to have been jinxed. Production was marred by technical problems and inefficiency on the part of the crew, and filming dragged on for almost a year, putting the movie millions of dollars over budget.

With Cicely Tyson as Cat. When *The Blue Bird* was released early in 1976, Jane found that a goodly portion of her performance had been left on the cutting-room floor: "I could have phoned in my part from Santa Monica!" She may not have minded, though, because the picture was thoroughly panned by the critics. Vincent Canby in the New York *Times:* "Mr. Cukor seems to have had less chance to direct in this case than to act as the goodwill ambassador who got his actors on and off the set in time. The English-language screenplay would try the patience of anyone . . . When Miss Fonda comes on, dressed in modified *Barbarella* gear as Night, I began to think she had written her own lines. Frets Night for no reason that has anything to do with the kiddie quest for the Bluebird, "What times we live in. I don't understand these last few years." Night sounds as if she had been moonlighting in the America of the Nixon administration."

The Blue Bird was Jane's fourth box-office fiasco in a row, and to many it was beginning to seem that her film career might be over. Instead, Jane was poised on the threshold of an unprecedented professional and personal comeback.

149

PART FIVE

COMEBACK
1977-79

Jane at the Cannes Film Festival in May 1978 to present the film that would win her a second Academy Award, *Coming Home.*

By early 1977, the war in Vietnam had been over for nearly four years—and so, for all intents and purposes, had Jane Fonda's career: she had not played a starring role in a major Hollywood movie in almost six years. But unlike the blacklistees of the McCarthy period—whose professional limbo lasted, in some cases, fifteen years—Jane had the good fortune to have dramatic, unprecedented political events unfold within just a few years that vindicated many of her positions.

The ignominious end of the war and the confirmation of many of the protesters' charges against the U.S. Government convinced all but the most diehard national chauvinists that the war had been a mistake; many came to believe the charge that the conflict had been entered into for immoral reasons.

But perhaps most important in establishing Jane as a woman who saw wrong and tried to right it, rather than as a shrill anti-American militant hurling unfounded accusations at her government, were the revelations of the Watergate hearings. For years Jane had accused President Richard Nixon of lying, covering up, wiretapping, and spying on American citizens. Fonda's attacks against Nixon had angered his supporters as much as her antiwar activities.

Everything changed, though, during the summer of 1974, when Richard Nixon—who had been reelected by the largest popular margin in history less than two years earlier—was forced to resign the presidency to avoid impeachment for "high crimes and misdemeanors." In June of 1972 a burglary at the offices of the Democratic National Committee was interrupted by security guards, setting in motion a series of events that revealed high-level chicanery unprecedented in American history: Nixon campaign operatives had, among other things, played "dirty tricks" on political opponents, burglarized offices, wiretapped, intercepted mail, and laundered money to cover up illegal contributions. Once the Watergate burglary was discovered, Nixon himself authorized a massive cover-up from inside the White House, including the payment of hush money and the destruction of evidence. As the Senate Watergate hearings uncovered more and more official criminality, Nixon unwaveringly denied charge after charge on national television. Many gave him the benefit of the doubt until he was forced by the Supreme Court to turn over audio tapes he had made of his White House conversations. The tapes—despite erasures and creatively edited "transcripts"—proved that Nixon had directly authorized the cover-up. When the House Judiciary Committee voted two bills of impeachment against Nixon, he resigned.

The American people were stunned. Their government was in disgrace, and from that point on few Americans would take at face value everything told to them by their leaders, and even fewer would assume that simply because the President supports a course of action it is the correct one. Americans became much more skeptical about many of the most cherished traditions of their country—traditions which Jane Fonda and many others were saying discriminated against the poor, minorities, women, gays, dissenters.

It was in this climate that the rehabilitation of Jane Fonda's reputation began. Of course, there were those who would never forgive her for her antiwar activities, especially her trip to Hanoi. Referring to the fact that she would forever remain "Hanoi Jane" to many Americans, she said: "I regret it very much, and I hope that in time people will understand that those were not my sentiments. When I did the things that were the most controversial, it was during the time Nixon was running for reelection as a 'peace candidate,' promising he would end the war. Those of us who were following the campaign intimately knew, as the international press knew, that he was escalating the war with the most extreme violence . . . I understand why people reacted the way they did and that's why I held off going [to Hanoi] for so long. Although the misunderstanding on the part of some people will probably be with me all my life, I don't regret going at all. I'm proud I did. And I don't view it as being pro Vietcong. I was an antiwar activist in a country whose government was *lying*."

With the redirection of Jane's political energies into economic programs designed to help renters, the poor, and exploited workers, many came to see her as a populist rather than a traitor. In 1976, film scripts started to come her way again, and her extraordinary screen presence and acting talent further redefined the public's impression of her. Starting with a light movie comedy, Jane's comeback would be accomplished with dizzying speed—and eventually not only reestablish her as one of Hollywood's biggest stars but—surprisingly—cause her to become one of America's most admired women.

OPPOSITE At the March 1977 American Film Institute Tribute to Bette Davis, Jane—the evening's host—presents Bette with the AFI Award. Jane had been born during the filming of *Jezebel*, in which her father costarred with Davis, and Jane told the audience, "My connection with Bette Davis is a little oblique. During the filming of *Jezebel*, my father's contract guaranteed that he would be through with his job and back in New York in time for my birth. What this must have caused in the way of problems for the actors and the director and the writers I cannot imagine." Davis, in fact, was made to perform some of her most important lines without Henry Fonda opposite her when he left before filming ended to be in New York for Jane's birth. "But," Jane concluded, "Bette Davis won her second Academy Award in spite of what I unintentionally put her through."

George Segal as Dick, and Fonda as Jane in the 1977 comedy *Fun with Dick and Jane,* the film that helped reestablish Jane Fonda as a major movie star in America. It was the tale of an affluent suburban couple whose life is turned upside down when he loses his job because of the sagging economy. Everything they own was bought on credit, and before long even their lawn is repossessed. Dick is overqualified for all available jobs, and Jane's attempts to work are disastrous—so they decide to become outlaws, robbing everything from supermarkets to the phone company (as fed-up customers cheer them on).

OPPOSITE Jane's first job as a restaurant fashion model ends in disaster. Fonda was paid a meager hundred thousand dollars to appear in *Fun with Dick and Jane,* and she accepted second billing to George Segal. She wanted to make the film, she said, "to show that I could still be pretty and still had a sense of humor." She achieved both goals admirably: audiences that had become accustomed to a hardbitten, shrill, humorless image of Jane Fonda were pleasantly surprised by her beauty, elegance, sexiness, and sense of fun in this film.

154

Three comic moments from *Fun with Dick and Jane*. The film was a major box-office success—and that success was directly attributable to Fonda. Overnight she was once again "bankable" in Hollywood, as a wave of publicity surrounding the film trumpeted the rather surprising fact that America had "fallen in love with Jane Fonda again." Vincent Canby's review noted, "I never have trouble remembering that Miss Fonda is a fine dramatic actress but I'm surprised all over again every time I see her do comedy with the mixture of comic intelligence and abandon she shows here. One sequence in particular, in which she makes a botch of an attempt at fashion modelling in a crowded restaurant, is a nearly priceless piece of modern slapstick."

Jane saw *Fun with Dick and Jane* as a message movie about the evils of rampant consumerism, and in many ways it was. But it differed from her earlier "message" films in one major respect: it was entertaining. After *Tout Va Bien*, Jane had pledged to herself that if she were going to make socially relevant movies, they would first have to be topflight entertainment. It was a credo that would serve her well over the next few years.

Jane proudly displays her Golden Apple Award, given by the Hollywood Women's Press Association to the movie personality deemed "most cooperative" with the press, December 1977. The award was especially meaningful to Fonda because the same organization had, just five years earlier, given her its *Sour Apple Award* for "presenting the worst image of Hollywood to the world." And, in still another example of the altered climate surrounding Jane, the award was presented to her by none other than John Wayne, one of the most vocal supporters of the United States military effort in Southeast Asia.

ABOVE RIGHT Peter and Jane congratulate their father as he receives the American Film Institute's Life Achievement Award at a banquet in Beverly Hills on February 28, 1978. Both of Henry Fonda's children had forged a tentative reconciliation with their father; although they were no happier about his difficulty in communicating with them than before, they were, as mature adults, better able to accept the man for what he was and forgive him for what he wasn't. Still, it would be another three years before Jane was fully able to come to terms with her feelings toward her father.

OPPOSITE Fonda as Lillian Hellman in Fred Zinnemann's film *Julia,* based on a story in Hellman's memoir *Pentimento.* Jane had wanted to play the role since first reading the book: Lillian, a young playwright, meets Julia, a young woman of deep political commitment, and they develop a warmly affectionate relationship. After a long separation, Lillian visits Paris in the mid-1930s and learns that Julia has been severely beaten by Nazi thugs at an anti-Hitler demonstration. She goes to the hospital, and is appalled by Julia's condition. The next day, she learns that Julia has been taken away by the Jewish underground to protect her life. Lillian is then approached on behalf of Julia and asked to smuggle fifty thousand dollars into Berlin for the purchase of exit visas for thousands of Jews. At great peril to herself, she does so, and her final moments with Julia are during a muted, dangerous meeting in a Berlin cafe.

Zinnemann agreed to Jane's request that Vanessa Redgrave be cast as Julia. Producer Richard Roth was all for it: "Why not? It was perfect symmetry. The two most famous left-wing women of the seventies playing two left-wing women of the thirties. I liked it. Of course, the fact that Jane and Vanessa were both terrific actresses didn't hurt either. Not to mention that they both agreed to work cheap."

Lillian and Julia develop a caring relationship soon after their meeting. *Julia* was unique in its depiction of a strong relationship between two females. During the seventies, good roles for women became extremely scarce; the male "buddy film" was at the height of its popularity. *Julia* helped popularize once again the "women's picture," and in fact took it several steps further. In a celebrated (and controversial) scene, Lillian tells Julia—as they lay bathed in romantic firelight—"I love you." Feminists decried what they saw as Zinnemann's too literal interpretation of the scene and the line, stressing that the love expressed was spiritual and platonic. In any event, Jane was thrilled. "Oh, to be able to play in scenes with another woman!" she exclaimed. "People will see a movie about women who think and who care for each other . . . In every other movie I've ever done

. . . [the woman] is either falling in or out of love or worried that she's going to lose a man. She's always defined in relationship to a man."

OPPOSITE With Jason Robards as Dashiell Hammett, the most important man in Lillian Hellman's life. Hammett's low-key encouragement of Hellman's activities and his stubborn prodding of her writing talent were other key elements of *Julia*. For Jane, recreating a living human being on screen—especially one as complex as Lillian Hellman—was one of her greatest challenges. "Lillian is a homely woman," she said, "and yet she moves as if she were Marilyn Monroe . . . She's a very sexual, sensual woman. That's fine for Lillian, but it wouldn't look right if I did it. So I played her more ascetic than she really is."

The final meeting between Julia and Lillian in a Berlin cafe. *Julia* was widely hailed as a brilliant, important motion picture, and its actors were uniformly praised. "Jane Fonda is so good as Lillian that it is almost embarrassing to watch her," wrote Norma McLain Stoop in *After Dark*. "One feels like a trespasser in the privacy of a life. Whether throwing her typewriter out the window of a Long Island beach cottage in despair at the progress of her play, holding the bruised hand of bandage-swathed Julia in a hospital in Vienna, slapping the face of a drunken New York friend who questions her relationship with Julia, trying to accustom herself to intrigue on the German border in the Hitler era or loving and screaming at the patient, supportive Hammett, she never loses a radiance born not only from talent but from self. Fonda gives what is unquestionably the finest film performance of any woman this year."

Richard Burton receives assistance lighting his cigarette from Jane and Peter O'Toole as Marsha Mason looks on, following the January 1978 Golden Globe Awards. Burton and Fonda were chosen as the Best Actor and Actress in a Drama for 1977 (he for *Equus*), but neither went on to win the Oscar. *Julia* was nominated in five of the top six Academy Award categories, but Jane and the film were edged out by Diane Keaton and *Annie Hall*. Jason Robards and Vanessa Redgrave were chosen as Best Supporting Actor and Actress. In an echo of Jane's award for *Klute*, there was some concern that Redgrave would politicize the ceremonies because of her strong pro-Palestinian views. While pro-Israel pickets demonstrated against Redgrave at the Music Center in downtown Los Angeles, she accepted the award and thanked the Academy for having the courage to give her the Oscar in spite of the attempts of "Zionist hoodlums" to prevent it. Redgrave's comment cast a pall over the proceedings and was viewed by most as totally inappropriate. Jane, in fact, was said to have further resolved to soften her public stands because she found Redgrave's manic political intensity and close-mindedness almost frightening. Redgrave's actions at the Oscar show—and the subsequent bitter controversy over her casting as a concentration-camp survivor in *Playing for Time*—ended her acting career in Hollywood for the next seven years. But in 1985 she was again Oscar-nominated, this time as Best Actress, for *The Bostonians*. Like Jane, Vanessa Redgrave is too talented to be denied work—and recognition—for very long.

Jon Voight and Jane as the tormented lovers in Hal Ashby's film *Coming Home*. Following *Julia*, Jane formed her own production company, IPC Films (for Indochina Peace Campaign), in association with Bruce Gilbert, an old friend from her protest days. Another old friend, Nancy Dowd, had written a tale of two women and their adjustment to life during the Vietnam War as they work in a veterans' hospital. Jane and Gilbert felt it would be more involving for general audiences if it were about a man and a woman, and they hired Waldo Salt and Robert C. Jones to rework the script. The final story revolved around the unliberated wife of a Marine Corps Captain who is left behind as her husband—a macho superpatriot—puts in for another tour of duty in Vietnam. Sally Hyde volunteers to work in a veterans' hospital, where she meets Luke Martin, a paraplegic who turns out to be a former high school classmate. Slowly she is drawn to him and—despite tremendous guilt on both their parts—they fall in love; their lovemaking leaves Sally sexually fulfilled

for the first time despite Luke's handicap because he, unlike her husband, is concerned with her satisfaction. Captain Hyde returns to find his wife questioning all his values—and sleeping with a paraplegic; after threatening them both with a bayonet, he drowns himself in the ocean.

OPPOSITE With Bruce Dern as her husband. *Coming Home* was considered a big risk for Jane by all involved; there was a great deal of fear that her antiwar activities would create a backlash against the film, or at the very least reignite some of the smoldering resentments against her. But Jane hoped that her characterization of Sally Hyde would mute the negative reaction. "The degree to which I can render that woman real has a whole political implication for me personally," she said, "because those are the kinds of people who hate me, who thought I was a traitor. Remember, there are still a lot of people out there who would like to see me dead."

With much trepidation, Sally and Luke consummate their love. To gauge the reaction of "my toughest audience," *Coming Home* producer Jerome Hellman screened the film for a group of representatives from veterans' organizations. As *American Film* described it, "It was warm, favorable, moving. One young man in a wheelchair, groping for words, said the film had caught the experience of the paraplegic. Hellman stayed an hour longer than he planned; he left with one paraplegic marine's grudging good wishes to Jane Fonda."

OPPOSITE The public's response to *Coming Home* was immediate and positive: it became a huge hit and won widespread critical acclaim. *Time* noted: "Though the illicit affair of a beautiful woman and a cripple is potentially maudlin stuff, Ashby does not allow his story to become overly sentimental. He does not view the couple's relationship as a panacea for all their emotional problems and he refuses to shy away from harsh detail . . . Fonda, though unconvincing in Sally's preliberation scenes, ultimately brings her character's horrifying internal conflicts to the surface. At such moments *Coming Home* reminds us of the choices everybody made during those harrowing war years—and of the price the nation paid thereafter."

Fall 1978: Jane looks lovingly at son Troy, five, as she relaxes at the Santa Barbara, California, ranch she and Tom Hayden had recently bought. In addition to housing the Hayden family, the ranch contained an educational center, set up by the Campaign for Economic Democracy, for underprivileged minority children—a place, Jane said, "to teach these kids how to lift themselves up from their bootstraps and lead the social revolution that is so long overdue in this state." Critics charged that Jane and Tom were "conditioning" children to think like them and become potential Hayden voters. Jane retorted to journalist Thomas Kiernan, "That's just plain B.S. We are teaching these young people how to organize their communities for themselves, not for Tom. The things people will invent!"

OPPOSITE Fonda as tough, fiercely independent rancher Ella Connors in *Comes a Horseman*, directed by Alan J. Pakula and released September 1978. Jane was attracted to this traditional Western because of its intriguing role reversal and Ella's struggle to keep her land from being taken, first by a greedy cattle tycoon (played by Jason Robards), then by a greedy oil company. Although Ella loses her fight against the oil company, Jane felt the film had an important message: there is strength in political numbers. "What should have happened," she offered, "is that all the small ranchers in the valley should have organized and banded together. Then, maybe, we would have won."

ABOVE LEFT Ella howls with rage as she and her lover Frank (James Caan) watch the takeover of her land. Caan's character comes into Ella's life after her struggle begins, and he helps her fight the corporate interests—and awakens her to romance. But the movie is all Fonda's, both in the writing and the performing. Director Pakula acknowledges the weighting of the film in favor of the female character: "In most Westerns," he says, "the woman is in a calico dress, running after the hero on the horse saying, 'Nothing is worth dying for,' or she's a gun-toting Calamity Jane. The idea of dealing with a heroine in the West, very much a woman yet willing to fight with the same passion as men, was a great attraction. I thought there was no one better than Jane Fonda to represent that kind of strong yet vulnerable American woman."

ABOVE RIGHT Pakula on location with Jane. Most critics agreed with his assessment; although many disliked the film, calling it "tedious," "hard to figure," "a quirkily interesting but unsuccessful work," they almost unanimously praised Fonda. *Time*'s review noted, "Pakula seems incapable of visual sloppiness or vulgarity. He has also coaxed a performance from Fonda that is superior to her rather saintly appearances in *Julia* and *Coming Home*. Her face as weather-beaten as her dad's in *The Grapes of Wrath*, this beautiful woman manages to capture the essence of frontier toughness in the film's first half. When she finally melts for a man, Fonda's blushing radiance almost melts a movie that has long since congealed."

171

As Hannah Warren in one of four segments in the film version of Neil Simon's broadway hit *California Suite,* directed by Herbert Ross. Hannah is a cynical, intense, elitist editor of *Newsweek* who comes to California to rescue her daughter from the West Coast life-style she has been sharing with her father, Hannah's ex-husband. The patented Simon one-liners were very much in evidence: "I can't wait to get out of here," Hannah says. "It's like Paradise with a lobotomy." Her husband explains why he enjoys the life-style: "I gave up my analyst. I went sane."

Despite long-standing criticisms of Simon's frequent glibness, Jane was anxious to do the film because she saw Simon's writing rather as "the kind of quick repartee that harkens back to the bright, brittle screen comedies of the good old days. But there's more to it than that. Seriousness underlies it, giving people something to think about. It has depth. I wouldn't have done it if this were just a string of gags or slapstick."

The climactic scene of Fonda's segment: Hannah and her ex depart after she realizes that her daughter wants to stay with her father and she has no right to force her to return to New York. Jane enjoyed working with Alan Alda: "I had never before known a man who called himself a feminist. We got along great."

California Suite was a Christmas release, Fonda's third 1978 film. It was a box-office winner, despite negative criticism of half the film: only Jane's segment and one starring Maggie Smith and Michael Caine as an Oscar nominee and her homosexual husband were generally well reviewed. *Time* said, "Jane Fonda and Alan Alda fare only fairly in their sketch . . . After exchanging some worn New York vs. Los Angeles one-liners, far inferior to Woody Allen's in *Annie Hall*, Fonda and Alda get all bittersweet . . . The superficial writing is not helped by Alda's unprepossessing screen presence, Ross' melodramatic use of close-ups or by a gratuitous beach scene that exists only to show off Fonda in a bikini."

But Stephen Farber in *New West* wrote, "Although Hannah isn't easy to like, she comes alive as one of the most vivid characters that Simon has ever created. Of course, he's lucky to have Jane Fonda inter-preting his lines. This amazing actress gives her third superb performance of 1978. She conveys the restless intelligence and the offputting arrogance of a New York journalist, and she also illuminates the fears that underlie Hannah's brittle, bitchy façade. This episode is uncharacteristic of Simon; it's scintillating, poignant and thoroughly compelling."

OPPOSITE With director Ross on location for a beach scene. The character of Hannah provided her, Jane says, with "the challenge of playing a woman I didn't like, who was very different from me." Then she added, "She's a type I'm afraid people think I'm really like, so there's a tendency to put a distance between her and myself, and that's no good. It was so demanding it scared me to death . . ."

This beach scene elicited some comment about Jane's figure, still sensational at forty. She commented, "I've been doing ballet for twenty years or so. I try to spend an hour a day exercising hard. The result is that I have a smaller waist now than when I was around twenty." Of course, Jane's body—and her workout regimen—would become extremely publicized before too much longer.

Happily clutching their Oscars, Jon Voight and Jane beam as they are named Best Actor and Best Actress of 1978 for their performances in *Coming Home.* Jane, much more emotional than she had been in 1972, expressed how important the film had been to her: "I wanted to win very much because I'm so proud of *Coming Home* and I want many people to see the movie." She delivered her speech in sign language as well as verbally: "I'm signing part of what I'm saying tonight because while we were making the movie, we all became more aware of the problems of the handicapped. Over fourteen million people are deaf." After thanking her coworkers, Jane added, "I want to thank my children, Troy and Vanessa, for being understanding and forgiving me my absences—and again, my husband . . . he helped me believe that besides being entertaining, movies can inspire and teach and even be healing. Thank you all very much."

Voight, winning his first Oscar, tearfully thanked Jane, "whose great dignity as a human being is very moving to me."

Jane's second Oscar—and the fact that it was for a role in a Vietnam-themed movie—signaled her total reacceptance by the American mainstream. In just two years, she had accomplished an unprecedented comeback—but even that would pale in comparison to her establishment as a popular-culture phenomenon over the next six years.

PART SIX

PHENOMENON
1979-85

Jane at her most beautiful and elegant in the 1981
film *Rollover*.

With Jane's Oscar for *Coming Home*, her reemergence as a major movie star was complete. Her extraordinary talent, beauty, and charisma had won over many Americans; in some cases, even those who opposed her political views granted her grudging respect and admiration for her considerable attributes.

But by the early 1980s, the extent of Jane's reacceptance by the American people would border on the phenomenal. She would become the most politically influential actress in history by funneling millions of dollars into her husband's Campaign for Economic Democracy, and stamp an indelible mark on American society in an area totally unrelated to anything she had previously espoused—health and fitness.

The erstwhile sex kitten and political radical became a businesswoman when she decided to produce her own films. "I'm interested in political films," she said. "But I'm not interested in turning audiences off. I want to turn them on. Not convert them, necessarily, but turn them on, make them think. As far as I'm concerned, any movie that tells the truth is a political film, only because most films don't tell the truth, or even try to."

In the don't-take-chances, politics-is-death mentality of Hollywood, Fonda was forced to produce her own films if she wanted to get them made at all. The concept was risky, the results far from certain. But Fonda's success with controversial, risky-themed films wasn't just acceptable, it was extraordinary: by 1984, the five films produced by Fonda's IPC Films had grossed over $340 million.

Jane had proven in the early seventies that she had her finger on the pulse of a large segment of America. In the early eighties, she did it again; it was a different segment, in a different context, and this time her finger had the Midas touch. Many of the hippies of the sixties and seventies had become the affluent "Me Generation," raising families and turning their antiwar consciousness to self-improvement, health foods, solar energy, nuclear disarmament. Jane was in the vanguard of this new social movement, and once again it was the result of her own personal evolution.

Jane had always appeared fit, always had a terrific figure—but it was achieved, she admits, in the worst possible way: she was, for fifteen years, bulimic. A lover of food, she would binge, then force herself to vomit so that she wouldn't gain weight. In the seventies, she conquered the problem, gave up red meat and fats, and began a strenuous exercise program which gave her a better body at forty than she had had at twenty.

Characteristically, Jane wanted to share her new self-awareness with others—and she wanted to raise money for Tom Hayden's Campaign for Economic Democracy. She invested in a health club, calling it "Jane Fonda's Workout," and developed a grueling regimen to get people back into shape. The results proved once again that when it comes to understanding the psyche of America, Jane Fonda may be prescient.

The Workout salon's success was such that it spawned two others, which together gross $2 million a year. Discouraged from franchising, Jane instead put together a book and videocassette for home use of the Workout. The book sold over two million copies in hardcover at $19.95, and earned Jane the biggest royalty check in Simon and Schuster's history: $2 million. The videocassette has sold half a million copies at $60.00 each, making it the biggest-selling videotape in history and earning Jane almost $4 million. Other spinoffs of the Fonda Workout—a pregnancy workout book and video, fitness calendars, a line of workout clothes, and her latest bestseller, *Women Coming of Age*, will earn Jane another $4–5 million.

By 1984, Jane Fonda was being called by *American Health* magazine "the godmother to the health/dance movement all over the world," a woman who has "probably already helped more people sweat off more fat pounds than anyone in history." She became a guru to millions, many of whom had fervently disagreed with her politics in the early 1970s.

Equally important in the resurgence of affection for Jane Fonda, perhaps, has been her political evolution. Although she has never apologized for her actions, she has softened. She admitted to Erica Jong that much of the time she didn't really have a handle on what she was saying, and that her approach had been wrong: "I wasn't a revolutionary. It would have been a lot better, I think, had I said, 'Look, folks, I am trying to develop expertise in this area,' and in the end I *was* an expert in many areas about the war, but in the beginning, I was strident. Instead of saying, '*Barbarella* is playing down the block, and it may seem pretty preposterous that I'm standing here talking about the war,' I was on soapboxes . . ."

Jane's political causes had evolved to encompass areas many average Americans were concerned about: renters' rights, energy conservation, sensible toxic-waste removal, avoidance of nuclear war. No longer was she seen as a dangerous radical by most, but as a woman with a social conscience who wanted to do something to improve the lot of millions of Americans. And she had the wherewithal to do it: millions of dollars of her Workout earnings have been donated to the Campaign for Economic Democracy to effect the changes Jane was calling for. She was seen as a woman willing to put her money where her mouth was, and she was saying things now that almost all of America could relate to.

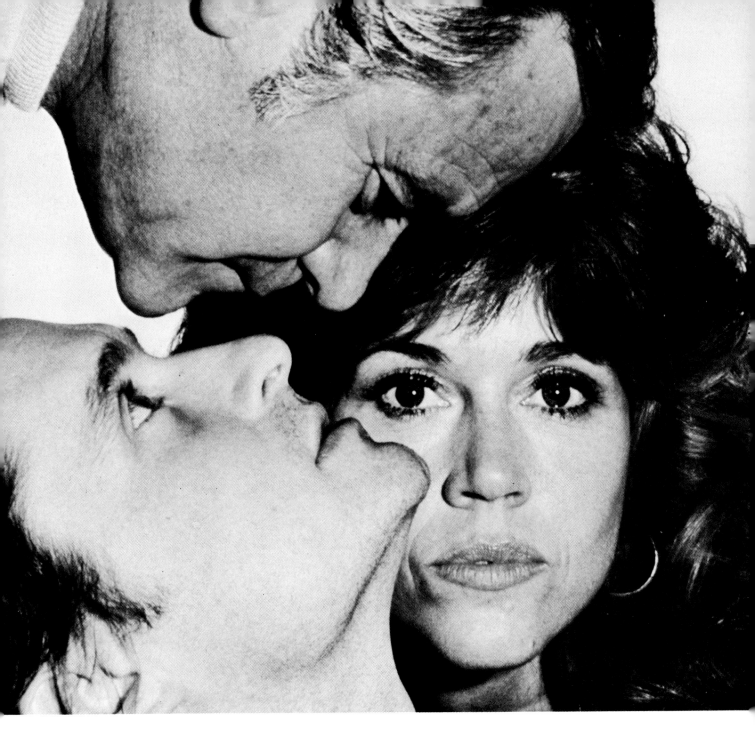

Fonda, Jack Lemmon, and Michael Douglas in an unusual publicity portrait from *The China Syndrome*, destined to become one of the most socially relevant films ever released. Television reporter Kimberly Wells (Jane) is sent on a routine story at a nuclear power plant, along with cameraman Richard Adams (Michael Douglas). While there, they witness a nuclear accident, which releases radioactive steam into the air and for a time threatens a "meltdown," which would result in widespread devastation.

Plant manager Jack Godell (Jack Lemmon), a company man always convinced his plant was safe, realizes that it in fact poses a grave threat to the entire community. He also comes to learn that the company has been falsifying documents that supposedly "prove" the plant's invincibility. At Wells's urging, he agrees to deliver his evidence to her, but he is nearly killed by company hit-men out to prevent it. In desperation, Godell takes over the plant by force and allows no one in the control room except Wells. A SWAT team bursts in and shoots Godell—whom the company has characterized as a dangerous lunatic. Finally, Wells is convinced by Godell's coworkers that he was correct about the dangers and the company cover-up, and, choking back tears, she broadcasts what she has learned.

OPPOSITE Kimberly reports from the nuclear power plant. Jane had opposed the proliferation of nuclear power after learning of the epidemic outbreak of cancer in St. George, Utah, as a result of nuclear-bomb testing there in the early sixties.

She also heard horrifying accounts of narrowly averted nuclear accidents, corporate cover-ups, and shoddy work standards at nuclear power plants. She wanted to do a film exposing the dangers and the duplicity, and attempted—unsuccessfully—to obtain rights to the Karen Silkwood story (it was later filmed with Meryl Streep). She read a script by director-screenwriter James Bridges that—for the sake of dramatic impact—combined many of the disparate stories of nuclear chicanery into one, and she liked it. But there was no role for a woman, so Bridges rewrote his reporter (originally to have been played by Richard Dreyfuss), and Fonda agreed to do the picture, with Bridges as director.

Director Bridges (in plaid jacket) helps lift Jane onto a stretcher after she fractured her right foot while filming a scene in which she ran down a rocky path. Jane was forced to wear a cast and walk on crutches, but fortunately the accident occurred close to the end of filming and it was possible for Bridges to camouflage Jane's infirmity.

The subject matter of *The China Syndrome* was kept secret from the public and much of the press. In order to gain access to a nuclear power facility, the producers had to lie, telling the power companies, "We aren't going to kick nuclear energy in the ass." But when word got out about the script, the workers at one facility began yelling at Jane, calling her a "pinko." "We were worried all day long," Jack Lemmon said.

183

Kimberly Wells Li
Ventana Power

OPPOSITE Kimberly tearfully tells the world that Jack Godell "wasn't a crazyman." When *The China Syndrome* was released in March 1979, it received high critical marks for its thrilling suspense and superb acting, but was taken to task by many for the "implausibility" of its premise. Nuclear power companies sent out a massive mailing to film reviewers prior to the movie's release, charging that it contained lies and inaccuracies, would unduly alarm the public and was doing a disservice to everyone. After the movie opened, power company executives called it "ridiculous," and the Edison Electric Institute claimed that "radioactive steam would be captured by the reactor's containment dome." Even *Time* critic Richard Schickel took the filmmakers to task: "The film depicts the utility company that owns the plant and the contractor that built it resorting to lies, corruption and violence to prevent the public from discovering how narrowly a disaster was averted . . . and never mind the sizable body of scientific opinion about the improbability of a chain of accidents anything like that posited in the film."

ABOVE Lemmon and Fonda attend the New York premiere. Within two weeks of its release, *The China Syndrome* went from a popular, controversial entertainment to a film of unprecedented prophecy. On March 28, 1979, a small valve misfunction at the nuclear power plant at Three Mile Island, near Harrisburg, Pennsylvania, allowed radioactive steam to escape into the atmosphere. At first officials of the power company, the state and the Nuclear Regulatory Agency stressed that it was a minor problem, with minimal radiation leakage, and that there was no need for panic. But within forty-eight hours, large-scale evacuations were taking place: a catastrophic core meltdown was imminent, necessitating the release of huge amounts of radioactive steam to prevent it. Suddenly, America and the world was confronted by the tremendous threat to life and health posed by nuclear-power plants, and many people were stunned not only by the emptiness of official reassurances but by the clear fact that the "experts" had little more knowledge of what would happen than the man in the street.

Three Mile Island turned *The China Syndrome* into a vitally important blockbuster film, and the filmmakers' prescience wasn't lost on the public. After *Time* and *Newsweek* featured cover stories on the film and the Three Mile Island accident, a letter writer reacted to a *Newsweek* column published before the accident: "I read with interest George F. Will's attack on Jane Fonda's film *The China Syndrome,* which included an accusation that Fonda had invented nuclear fantasies about melting cores in the interest of satisfying her own greed," wrote Robert Rodi of Illinois. "However, Will had the misfortune of having his piece see print during the same week that the Harrisburg incident reared its ugly head. We Americans are notoriously thickheaded, but must even the journalists of this country have to relearn the hard lesson that Jane Fonda is usually right?"

185

The lighter side of Jane Fonda is showcased on a Helen Reddy television special aired May 22, 1979. Jane played an actress who, accepting an award, vehemently lashes out against all those people who hindered her rise to the top. She will not be silenced, until one of the presenters—played by Elliott Gould—tries to remove her forcibly from the stage. Jane also made her singing debut on this show.

OPPOSITE May 6, 1979: Jane and Tom take part in a march on Washington to protest against the building and activating of nuclear power plants. Chanting "No more Harrisburgs," the crowd heard Jane, California Governor Jerry Brown, Ralph Nader, and others warn that the Three Mile Island emergency might not remain an isolated incident.

Henry and Jane sit for an interview by Tom Brokaw for "The Today Show," aired May 30 and 31, 1979. Brokaw asked Henry if he could have been happily married to a woman like Jane. "You mean an activist?" Henry replied. "I think so." Jane added, "I don't know about living happily, but we could have had a good affair." Jane remembered having been "terrified" of her father's "rages" when she was a little girl, and she admitted that their renowned lack of communication hadn't improved much. "A lot of how my dad feels about me I read in the press," she said.

Over three hundred of Jane's colleagues took out a full-page ad decrying the Senate's action: "Whether or not we agree with Jane Fonda's personal views, we all agree that she is an American who cares passionately about the pressing issues which have and continue to face our country. What is at stake is not the civil liberties of one woman but the rights of all of us . . . We affirm that we will fight any resurrection of the spectre of McCarthyism in California or our nation."

The legislators refused to budge, and Jane withdrew from contention.

ABOVE RIGHT California Governor Jerry Brown and Jane appear in the state capitol to denounce the legislature's veto of Brown's appointment of Jane to the State Arts Council. Citing her "acts of treason" during the Vietnam war, the legislature refused to allow her to serve in the nonpolitical capacity. Jane, Brown, and many others were incensed. Brown said the lawmakers "lacked the guts to let her at least come before the Senate and speak her mind." Jane tearfully noted that she was living in France during the early years of the Vietnam war. "It would have been easy for me to have stayed there and to have avoided the ensuing controversy. In my opinion, I became a patriot in the true sense of the word when I returned home and took the stand I did."

OPPOSITE Boston, September 28, 1979: Jane and Tom picket in support of the California United Farm Workers' Union call for a boycott of iceberg lettuce picked by non-union labor. The Haydens had embarked on what was dubbed by reporters "The Road Show for Economic Democracy"—a tour of fifty cities in which they campaigned for rent control, corporate control by employees, energy alternatives, and health care improvements, and against nuclear power, unfair working conditions, and corporate polluting. While a grass-roots stampede to their causes didn't take place, the Campaign for Economic Democracy already boasted seventeen ballot-box victories—most of them winning tougher rent-control laws.

OPPOSITE In her thirtieth film, *The Electric Horseman,* Jane once again played a television reporter, and costarred for the third time with Robert Redford. Director Sydney Pollack's film carried an anti-big-business, pro-ecology message in its story of Sonny Steele, a downtrodden ex-rodeo star (Redford) hired as a pitchman for a cereal. When he discovers during a Las Vegas convention appearance that the champion horse which represents the cereal's logo is being drugged to keep it docile, he kidnaps it in order to set it (and himself) free. Reporter Hallie Martin covers the story, and before long she joins Steele on the lam from police and corporate thugs, helps him achieve his aims and shares his bed.

Jane did not enjoy location shooting in Las Vegas. "It's a place built on greed, representing the absolute worst in our culture," she said. "The ethic that built this city is horrendous." Jane decided to see firsthand "the other side" of Las Vegas—"This is a boom town, but where do the maids live? There's the Strip, a wall, and a ghetto." One of the movie's themes—the amorality of advertising hype—was especially meaningful for Jane, who has always refused to endorse a product: "It makes me sad to see these people doing commercials. It's very clear that they're doing it for the money. I'm glad my dad isn't doing it anymore. [Henry Fonda represented GAF in the seventies.] Acting is a craft, we're artists and that should be kept separate from the pitching of goods."

ABOVE LEFT Sharing an intimate moment with Sonny, Hallie marvels at the numerous scars he has accumulated over the years in the violent world of the rodeo.

In order to get one seemingly uncomplicated kiss scene on film, Pollack was required to shoot forty-eight takes. As journalist George Haddad-Garcia put it, "That meant that poor Jane had to kiss Robert Redford forty-eight times, between nine A.M. on a Tuesday and six P.M. the next day." Seventy-five-hundred feet of film was shot, at a cost of $280,000. The film's cost accountant was heard to mutter, "It would have been cheaper if Redford had kissed the horse."

ABOVE RIGHT *The Electric Horseman* was a popular success—the biggest moneymaker of the 1979 fall movie season—but it received mixed reviews. Some praised the film as entertaining if inconsequential, but for the first time since her reemergence as a major movie star, Jane began to be criticized for the message content of her films. *Newsweek*'s Jack Kroll wrote: "Will we ever see Jane Fonda and Robert Redford playing unvirtuous people, people on the wrong side of the great issues, scurvy meanies, wrongos instead of rightos? Don't bet on it. That's too bad, because we need Lady MacBeths as well as Cordelias, Iagos as well as Othellos, and you'd think that high-voltage actors like Fonda and Redford would want to transmit both the negative and positive electricity in human beings . . . it's interesting that they seem to see themselves as behavioral models . . . if you'll only agree with them on whatever it is—the Vietnam war, nuclear energy, the environment—you too can have the golden flair and ethical sexiness of Fonda and Redford."

191

OPPOSITE Despite a broken foot—the result of an accident in her host's home—Jane continues a visit to the Wailing Wall in Jerusalem during a June 1980 trip to Israel. Tom, Vanessa, and Troy accompanied her on the visit, where she attended the opening of *The Electric Horseman* and participated in fundraisers for the Haifa Municipal Theater. Tom, as a member of California's SolarCal Council, visited with Israeli solar energy experts.

After visiting a kibbutz, Vanessa told Jane she wanted to stay and live there. By way of explanation, Jane wryly commented, "Children there live separately from their parents."

Reporters created near riots wherever Fonda went, prompting the extraordinary scene of Israeli police shooting out the tires of a car full of journalists trailing Fonda, and shooting into the air to scatter a horde of other newsmen following her. Only once did Jane herself publicly react to the hounding: when she visited a monument to Holocaust victims. "You won't even let me cry by myself!" she told the press.

ABOVE Fonda as Judy Bernly, a recent divorcee who takes her first job, as a secretary, in *Nine to Five*. Once again, Jane turned her concern over a particular social issue into mass entertainment—this time, it was the treatment of secretaries and other working women within the corporate structure. Jane, director Colin Higgins, and producer Bruce Gilbert all did on-the-scene research while putting the movie together. Jane reported: "Without exception, the women I spoke to *liked* their work . . . the problem isn't with the job so much as how management treats their secretaries, showing a lack of respect that reflects itself in wages, lack of promotion, and the menial tasks they're asked to do."

197

OPPOSITE Costars Lily Tomlin and Dolly Parton join Jane in a publicity photo for the film. Lily played Violet Newstead, the highly efficient manager of the secretarial staff, who is continually passed over for promotion in favor of men she herself has trained. Dolly portrayed the warmhearted, sexy-but-bright Doralee Rhodes, who must constantly outrun the lecherous advances of her boss, Mr. Hart (Dabney Coleman).

When Violet accidentally puts rat poison in Hart's coffee ("You think they're not going to fire me for something like that?"), a wild series of events is put into motion during which the three oppressed co-workers kidnap Hart (he didn't drink the coffee) and pretend that he has ordered sweeping reforms in the office (day-care centers, flexible hours, etc.). Finally, the corporation president, impressed by the increased morale and output of the revitalized staff, sends Hart to South America to do the same for the branch office there.

ABOVE The office revolutionaries celebrate victory over their boss at the conclusion of *Nine to Five*. The film, a fast and funny slapstick with wonderful perfor-

mances from all concerned, was an enormous hit upon its release in December 1980. Although in many ways too exaggerated and silly to have much of an impact as a "message" film, it did strike a nerve with millions of working people, as did the Number 1 hit title song, written by Dolly. Reviews were generally favorable (criticizing mostly the absurdity of some of the situations); several saw deeper meaning in the film than others. Nancy Scott of the San Francisco *Chronicle* wrote, "The heroes in farcical comedies like *Nine to Five* are traditionally foolish, likeable, put-upon characters, and they act for every one of us who has ever suffered working or dealing with authority. And they are traditionally men. I think this is the first time I have seen women who were allowed to be heroes *and* foolish. It's wonderful."

Meri Lyndon also commented, in *Hollywood Studio* magazine, "A pat on the back to Ms. Fonda, an actress whose skills improve with age (as do her remarkable looks), and who isn't content to take the scripts handed to her and simply pick out the best of the worst. As a feminist and a creative filmmaker, she is doing more for actresses, female characters and humanist entertainment than most of the studios put together."

December 14, 1980: Jane and Tom stand sadly silent during a Central Park vigil in memory of John Lennon, slain by a gunman outside his Manhattan apartment building. One hundred thousand people paid their respects to Lennon during the tribute, one of many held around the world.

ABOVE RIGHT Dolly and Jane join Lily Tomlin for a sketch on Lily's February 2, 1981, TV special "Lily: Sold Out." "I was helping put together one of the sketches for the show," Lily said, "and I thought it would be a great idea to include Jane Fonda. When I called her she was really enthusiastic about appearing with me. A few days later I got a call from Dolly, who said, 'How come I'm not in the show and Jane is?' So we wrote in a part for Dolly, too." The show got mixed reviews (with some critics singling out the Fonda sketch as a low point) but was a big ratings winner.

OPPOSITE Henry Fonda as Norman Thayer with Katharine Hepburn and Jane as his wife and daughter in *On Golden Pond,* the film version of Ernest Thompson's play. Jane purchased the film rights as a gift to her father, and it was clearly the perfect vehicle to unite them for the first time on screen: crusty, taciturn Norman returns to his summer house at Golden Pond for what will probably be the last time; he is in failing health. His wife Ethel struggles to keep him active and in good spirits. The visit of his daughter Chelsea creates tension; their relationship has long been strained by his inability to show affection and by Chelsea's rebellious reaction to that.

The parallels to the real-life relationship between Jane and Henry were obvious. "My dad isn't exactly Norman Thayer," Jane said, "but there's a lot of Dad in the part . . . Like Chelsea, I had to get over the desperate need I once had for his approval, and to conquer my fear of him. We've never been intimate. My dad simply is not an intimate person. But that doesn't mean there isn't love . . ."

OPPOSITE Working with Katharine Hepburn was for Jane almost as emotional an experience as working with her father. "To work with her, and to work with my father, was a terrifying, waking up in the morning wanting to throw up kind of experience . . . I couldn't help fantasizing what would have happened if she and my dad had become lovers forty years ago, and Kate had been my mother."

ABOVE The filming of *On Golden Pond* developed into a form of therapy for Jane and Henry. The relationship between Norman and Chelsea was so close to their own that the understanding the estranged father and his daughter come to in the film extended itself to the real people playing them. Jane was able without trouble to convey Chelsea's bitterness toward her father, by recalling memories of her own feelings toward Henry—and, on several occasions, experiencing them once again. Jane is an actress who needs a great deal of feedback from other actors, and for a closeup of Henry's, she offered to help by being there for him, so that he could maintain eye contact with her. "I don't need to see you," Henry snapped. "I'm not that kind of actor."

"I felt so invalidated," Jane said. "I was furious. I felt like crying. I'm forty-four years old and still he can reduce me to feeling abject helplessness." Still, she added, "the other side of me said, 'Great! These are the emotions Chelsea is feeling.'"

Another time, when Chelsea is confronted with her need to tell her father how she feels, Jane found the reality of it almost unbearable. It was Katharine Hepburn who helped her through the moment. As Jane explained to Barbara Walters: "It was the hardest scene I've ever done. And it became the actor's nightmare, because from the first moment we rehearsed it, all the way through the master and his close-up, I was so *full*. But when the time came for *my* close-up, I dried up—it was not there. I said to Katharine, 'I need help—and don't tell Dad.' She knew exactly what I meant. So she stood in the bushes behind me off camera, and I turned and looked into her eyes and she did this" [she indicates a "give to me" gesture] "and it was Katharine Hepburn to Jane Fonda saying, 'I know what this means to you and by God you *tell* him.' She *fed* me. I could feel it coming from her right into me. It was wonderful. At the end I said, 'I want to be your friend,' and I'll never forget it, because my dad was never very emotional—he didn't cry on camera or on stage. I touched him . . . I waited until his last close-up and he didn't expect it and I touched him and I could see the tears well up in his eyes . . ."

On location with director Mark Rydell. Another highly emotional aspect of filming *On Golden Pond* was its theme of an elderly couple having to face mortality, because Fonda himself was in failing health. "They approached this material bravely," Rydell said on the PBS-TV special *Starring Katharine Hepburn.* "Here you have Henry Fonda and Katharine Hepburn, both people in their seventies, dealing with material that has to do with the final years of one's life, and how do you face death and how do you support one another . . . it was quite a resonant experience."

OPPOSITE *On Golden Pond* proved to be quite a satisfying experience for audiences. The teaming of Henry with Kate and Jane touched America's heart, as did its themes of mortality and reconciliation with loved ones. The film became a huge hit, the biggest moneymaker of 1981. The reviews were mixed, many critics finding the film a manipulative tearjerker, but David

Ansen's opinion in *Newsweek* was closer to the general public's perception: "The story is sentimental. But call it what you may—middlebrow, manipulative— the movie lives and breathes and has the power to pluck a responsive chord in all but the most cynical viewer . . . of course, the main attraction is that resonant, once-in-a-lifetime cast . . . which automatically turns *On Golden Pond* into an event in movie star mythology. It's not just the Thayers we're reacting to, but five decades of movie memories. The movie shimmers in iconographic stardust."

On Golden Pond received six major Academy Award nominations: Best Picture, Best Actor, Best Actress, Best Director, Best Supporting Actress and Best Screenplay (Ernest Thompson). Hollywood was abuzz with speculation over whether Henry would win the first Oscar in his illustrious career, whether Kate could possibly win her *fourth,* and whether Jane would be named for the first time in the Supporting category. But the country would have to wait almost a year to find out.

Jane as the elegant, sophisticated former actress Lee Winters in *Rollover,* Alan J. Pakula's film about international high finance. At the height of her career, Lee gave up movies to marry the head of a chemical company. When he is killed, she wants to take over as chairman of the board. She meets Hub Smith (Kris Kristofferson), a troubleshooter hired by a big New York City bank to help it through a financial crisis. They team up to pull off a financial coup—gaining an Arab loan—which will win Lee control of the company. While falling in love, they discover (separately) an Arab plot to siphon off millions of dollars for illegal purposes, a plot that involves the chemical company and the bank. People are killed, Lee is nearly kidnapped by her husband's murderer, and she and Hub come to suspect each other of involvement in the plot. Feeling betrayed, and desperate not to lose her company, Lee attempts to coerce the Arabs into giving her the money she needs by informing their representative that she knows of their illegal acts. They pull out billions of dollars from United States banks, devastating the world economy.

Once again, Jane's intent was to get a message across: "I think the most important development in our lifetime is what has happened to energy and the fact that small Arab countries which have oil are calling the shots in relation to our energy and our flow of money. In other words, they have power over our future. It's an issue that hasn't been dealt with seriously except in a few books."

FOLLOWING PAGE Kris Kristofferson and Jane film a touch-football scene on location. Kris wasn't sure he wanted to do the film—he was uncomfortable in a suit, and he didn't want to shave his beard off. "I used it as a protective mask," he said. "I felt naked without it—terribly exposed. The fact is, I wasn't right for the film, but Jane wanted me and I wanted to work with her and Alan. So I did it."

During filming, rumors arose of a romance between Jane and Kris—rumors published by the *National Enquirer,* along with photos of the couple on a "date." The reports, Jane said, were completely untrue. "This kind of thing has never happened to me before in my life," she said. "It took me by surprise, and it was embarrassing. Fortunately, Tom is who he is and we could just talk about it. It was hard to figure out what to do. You can't sue, because that just calls attention to it, so we just decided to forget about it."

Kristofferson said, "Those pictures of Jane and me —we weren't even together. Look at them! The worst thing about the rumors was that it changed the atmosphere a little for me. It wasn't as much fun, and we kind of lost an innocence. You know, you couldn't hold your friend's hand anymore, because that might be taken wrong . . ."

OPPOSITE When *Rollover* was released in December 1981, it proved to be a financial and critical disaster. Although Pakula gave the film much of the dramatic tension and suspense of his brilliant *All the President's Men*, and the filmmakers conquered their greatest challenge—to make the complicated world of high finance intelligible to the viewer—the film's characters and relationships proved strangely lifeless. There was some chemistry between Jane and Kris, but their love story was not an important enough element in the film to excite the audience's imagination. Many of the reviews were savage. Joy Gould Boyum wrote in *The Wall Street Journal:* "The only thing startling about *Rollover* is its total ineptitude. The muddled, foolish plot is filled with all sorts of financial wheelings and dealings and of various murders and a would-be kidnapping that are either ill-explained or unconvincing . . . the love scenes are wooden, or, more precisely, chilly . . . so perva-sive is the coldness among the super rich here that more than the Arab menace and the precarious financial situation, it seems to be the film's central point. After all, didn't we all grow up reading about Midas and the dehumanizing effects of greed? Ironically enough, Miss Fonda's stunning wardrobe, dazzling furs and elegant coiffures contradict that notion: they're the most entertaining and appealing thing in *Rollover.*" Audiences avoided the movie, making it the only financial flop that Jane's IPC Films had produced. The totality of its failure can be gauged by comparing its box-office receipts to other recent Fonda films: $103 million for *Nine to Five*, $101 million for *On Golden Pond*, $84 million for *The China Syndrome* and $50 million for *Coming Home. Rollover*'s take: $6 million.

But with *On Golden Pond* still in release and racking up the year's highest box-office grosses, Jane was still riding high professionally as she entered 1982.

In April 1982, Henry Fonda won his first Academy Award for Best Actor, and Katharine Hepburn won her fourth. A radiant and emotional Jane accepted the award for her father, who was too ill to attend the ceremonies. "Oh, Dad," she said, tears filling her eyes as she looked directly into the camera. "I'm so happy and proud for you . . . My father didn't really believe that this was going to happen—but he told me a while back that if it did, he wanted his wife, Shirlee, to accept the award for him. But Shirlee wanted to be with him tonight, as is her way, and so I'm here . . . I know that he's very, very honored and very happy and surprised—and I bet he said, 'Hey, ain't I lucky,' as though luck had anything to do with it . . . I know that he feels that he never would have won this if it hadn't been for Katharine Hepburn . . . and I know that lastly, but really first, he is thanking Shirlee Fonda, who he calls his 'Rock of Gibralter' . . . I think she's his Ethel Thayer. Dad, me and all the grandchildren are coming over with this right away!"

"It was, I think, the happiest night of my life," Jane

said. Backstage after picking up the award, Jane poses with her family: Left to right, Henry's adopted daughter, Amy; Peter's daughter, Bridgett; Troy Hayden; Tom; Vanessa Vadim.

OPPOSITE After the ceremonies ended, Jane rushed home to present her father with his award. He had blushed and cried as he listened to Jane's acceptance speech, but he confessed, "I wasn't really surprised. It was in the wind." Tom Hayden described the moment when Jane gave her father the Oscar: "It was very, very touching. He was so overwhelmed when Jane handed the Oscar to him, he couldn't say a word . . . he was just sitting there in a state of bemused shock with the Oscar resting in his lap."

"There's no question about it," Henry added, "this has to be one of the high points of my life. I'm really happy and I'm proud, and I'm particularly happy that Katharine won, and Ernest [Thompson], too."

Troy and Jane accompany Tom as he takes his seat in the California State Assembly in Sacramento, December 6, 1982. Tom won handily in his heavily Democratic district, completing a remarkable transformation from "dangerous radical" to people's representative. He quickly established a reputation as an effective fighter for his district and a champion of rent control, the elderly and the disenfranchised, and surprised many with his legislative ability and success at compromise. In 1984, he was reelected for another two-year term.

Cheerleading once again, Jane waves pom-poms as she and Tom attend Super Bowl XVIII in Tampa, Florida, rooting for the L.A. Raiders in their quest for the NFL championship versus the Washington Redskins. The Raiders won, 38–9.

Six weeks earlier, Jane had conducted a ninety-minute workout in her Beverly Hills club to refute rumors that she had suffered a heart attack. The story appeared first in the London *Daily Mail,* and was picked up in America by *USA Today.* Jane was angry that the story was repeated with no attempt to verify it with her, and that other papers in the United States picked it up after she denied it. She decided to publicly do a vigorous workout to reassure hundreds of friends and relatives who had flooded her with concerned telephone calls after reading the items. "I haven't even had a cold all this year," Jane said.

North Miami Beach, Florida, February 28, 1984: Jane makes an unscheduled appearance at Burdine's department store to promote her new line of workout clothes, designed to accompany her books and videocassettes. Two other stores in the area had canceled Fonda's appearances after protests from conservative groups—and a bomb threat against her. Her appearance at Burdine's was made without the knowledge of the store's owners. "I wasn't surprised by the protests," Jane said. "There are always a small group of extremists who are very vocal . . . what did surprise me was that the stores caved in to the pressure."

OPPOSITE In more liberal San Francisco, Jane's appearance at Macy's in March was a huge success. She insisted that her workout clothes be manufactured in the United States by union workers. A year after the line debuted, however, its manufacturer filed for bankruptcy, claiming that sales of the workout clothes were disappointing and put a financial strain on the company. It was the only workout-related enterprise that did not pan out for Jane—because, she says, she wasn't as personally involved as she usually is. "You've got a better chance to hit a home run, be successful, when you're in an area you understand. When I do something myself, like my book or tapes or movies, I do all right. But with the clothing, I didn't realize until too late that the management was making mistakes. I knew the clothes were good, but they also need to be delivered on time, placed correctly, all those things. I've learned a lot, and I'm convinced that, run properly, a Jane Fonda Workout line of exercise clothes will work."

218

Jane as Gertie Nevels in *The Dollmaker,* her first made-for-TV movie, aired May 13, 1984. She had wanted to play this character since 1971, when she first read Harriette Arnow's 1954 bestseller. The story is about a family of sharecroppers in the Kentucky hills who are uprooted when the husband gets a job in a Detroit factory. The move creates severe hardship—then terrible tragedy—for Gertie and her five children. The only thing that allows them to survive is Gertie's ability to carve beautiful dolls and figures out of wood—a talent which brings the family desperately needed money and Gertie a sense of her own self-worth. Here, Gertie loses herself in the completion of her most ambitious work, a large, Christ-like figure.

FOLLOWING PAGE Much was made of Jane's almost eerie resemblance to her father in this film. That wasn't the only similarity, according to Jane. "It was the first time this ever happened to me," she said. "All the way through the filming I would hear my voice come out of my mouth and it was *him.* I *heard* him."

Jane struggled for eight years to make a deal to film this story, and it wasn't until the day after her Oscar win for *Coming Home* that she got ABC to agree. "What were they going to say? I had just won my second Oscar [and] I wanted to do my first TV movie . . . They said yes."

"I loved Gertie's courage in the face of bone-and-soul-crushing experiences. I also loved her humility and her capacity for mothering. It's very rare to find a project that shows a woman doing the things that women do—raising children, nurturing, serving as the backbone of the family—without condescension or false feminization."

Jane's original desire to do *The Dollmaker* as a feature film gave way to her growing appreciation of the power of television, brought home by the phenomenon of *Roots.* "The impact that it had was extraordinary," Jane said. "You can write a poem or a haiku or make a forty-million-dollar movie, but when you do television, you have opportunities that you don't have anywhere else, and one of them is to reach masses of people."

221

Jane chats with Bill and Gertrude Cole, in whose Mount Vernon, Kentucky, home she stayed while filming. After they completed their roles in *Nine to Five,* Dolly Parton took Jane deep into the mountains so that she could research for her role as Gertie. "Dolly was the first hillbilly I ever met," she said. "She took me on her tour bus . . . we chopped wood and I learned to milk a cow and churn butter and bake biscuits and learn the rhythm of the mountains." One couple in particular, Lucy and Waco Johnson, taught Jane what hard work really is: "I worked real hard with them. I'm in pretty good shape, but I spent one day doing what seventy-four-year-old Waco does every day . . . and at the end of the day I couldn't move. But that experience enriched the characterization." Jane adds: "It was one of the greatest experiences of my life."

ABOVE RIGHT Gertie comforts her daughter. Filming *The Dollmaker* was a highly personal, highly emotional experience for Jane. Director Daniel Petrie remembers vividly the final day of filming, when he turned to Jane and said, "Well, Miss Fonda, it's a wrap":

"Jane reached out and put her arm around me. And she sobbed for ten minutes. Her whole body was shaking. I think it was because the character was dead, and she was in mourning."

The Dollmaker received high ratings and excellent reviews. Martha Bayles in *The Wall Street Journal* complained about the opening sequences, which "automatically warmed my heart every 60 seconds or so—which I always resent. Why should such a valuable organ be treated like a giblet under a heat lamp?" But, "as the Nevels family struggled through their tragic winter in Detroit, I was thoroughly engrossed."

Bayles, as did many other critics, commented on Jane's similarity to her father in this film. "Miss Fonda has said that her father would have loved this film more than anything else she has done. I agree . . . It's impossible not to know about the famous Fonda generation gap. I will not speculate about the substance of the argument . . . but since style so often expresses substance in Hollywood, it seems that the final round must be awarded to the elder. After all, imitation is the sincerest form of capitulation."

Barbra Streisand poses with Jane after Fonda cochaired and cosponsored a National Organization of Women tribute to Streisand as their "Woman of Courage," June 6, 1984. Speculation of a Fonda/Streisand screen teaming has circulated for years, but to date nothing has been firmed up.

OPPOSITE Jane proudly holds her Emmy Award, presented to her as the Best Actress in a Drama for *The Dollmaker* in September 1984. Fonda told the audience, "You don't know how happy this makes me, because this project was very, very important to me."

Still vibrantly beautiful at forty-seven, Jane late in 1984 published her third book, *Women Coming of Age.* Pointing out that her mother, at forty, felt that her beauty and youth were gone, Jane stresses in this book her belief that fitness and the correct mental attitude can keep everyone youthful for far longer.

She would like to do a film about women getting older. "Hollywood is not forgiving of women with wrinkles," she told *American Health* magazine. "Most of the big actresses from the '50s and '40s and '30s would get right up where I am now, and then there'd be this huge hiatus. They disappear. If lucky, they come back later as character actresses. I want to help change that, so I want to play my age, show that a middle-aged woman can still be vibrant and sexually dynamic."

Jane's latest opportunity to prove that will come in late 1985, when the Norman Jewison film version of the Broadway hit *Agnes of God* is released. In it, Jane plays a sophisticated, irreligious psychiatrist called in to treat a young nun who has killed her newborn baby. Meg Tilly plays the tortured, confused nun, Agnes, and Anne Bancroft is the Mother Superior, whose main interest is in covering up the facts of the tragedy.

Clearly, Jane Fonda will continue to seek out important, controversial, and challenging film roles for as long as she makes movies. Even more clear is the fact that the passions and commitments of her life have in no way abated, and may in fact be stronger than ever. There are few certainties in life, but this must surely be one: for as long as she is able to speak out, Jane Fonda will be in the forefront of the most pressing social issues of her time. And the fact that her future stands will arouse controversy just as surely as did those she has taken over the past seventeen years is perhaps a large part of what keeps Jane Fonda fighting.

PHOTO CREDITS

Michael Abramson/Gamma 189
Bettmann Archive *iv, vi, 3(top), 6(left),* 13, 19*(top),*
    26*(top),* 32, 34
John Bryson/Sygma 211
Cindy Charles/Gamma 219
Robert Deutsch 144, 185
Nancy Ellison/Sygma 167
Jean-Claude Francolon/Gamma 196
Gamma-Liaison 87, 118, 128, 130, 136
Arthur Grace/Sygma 187
Philippe Ledru/Sygma *ii,* Color Plate 8
Jim MacHugh/Sygma 147
Benami Neumann/Gamma 214
Omaha *Times-Herald* 14
Pictorial Parade 11*(left),* 19*(bottom),* 26*(bottom),* 46,
    49, 51, 52, 54, 56, 64, 65, 92, 100, 116, 131,
    137*(top),* 138, 186
Steve Schapiro/Gamma 212
Steve Schapiro/Sygma *viii,* Color Plates 2, 3, 4, 6,
    and 7, 168, 192, 194
Robert Scott 132*(both),* 153, 158*(both),* 163*(bottom),*
    224, 225
Seattle *Times* 114
UPI/Bettmann Archive 15, 21, 41, 71, 119, 129, 141,
    193*(bottom)*
J. Watson Webb, Jr. *x,* 3*(bottom),* 4–5, 6*(right),* 7–9,
    12*(left)*
J. Watson Webb, Jr. Collection 10, 11*(right),* 12*(right)*
Wide World 104, 117, 140, 146, 183, 188*(both),*
    193*(top),* 200*(left),* 213*(both),* 215–218, 223*(left)*

ABOUT THE AUTHOR

James Spada has written ten books, including
*Streisand: The Woman and the Legend, Shirley and Warren,
The Divine Bette Midler, Judy and Liza, Hepburn: Her Life
in Pictures,* and *Monroe: Her Life in Pictures.*

A native New Yorker, he now lives in a mountain
cabin in Sky Forest, California, where he is at work on
his next book, *Grace: The Story of a Princess.*